# The Ultimate Fondue Cookbook for Beginners and amateurs:

**About 130 Delicious, Simple, and Creative Recipes of Sweet, Spicy, Dessert Fondue, and Much, Much More than You Can Cook Yourself and for Any Occasion.**

By **Max F. Falcon**

# Table of contents:

THE ULTIMATE FONDUE COOKBOOK FOR BEGINNERS AND AMATEURS:

ABOUT 130 DELICIOUS, SIMPLE, AND CREATIVE RECIPES OF SWEET, SPICY, DESSERT FONDUE, AND MUCH, MUCH MORE THAN YOU CAN COOK YOURSELF AND FOR ANY OCCASION.

| | |
|---|---|
| CHAPTER 1: A GRANDE MELT-RODUCTION TO FONDUE | 1 |
| 1.1. THE CHRONICLES OF CHEESE: A GOOEY TALE RETOLD | 1 |
| 1.2. FONDUE'S RICH PALETTE – A DIP INTO DIVERSITY | 1 |
| 1.3. THE FONDUE KIT CHRONICLES - TOOLS OF THE DIP TRADE | 2 |
| 1.4. "THE FONDUE SAFETY DANCE" | 3 |
| CHAPTER 2: THE FONDUE-VOLUTION OF INGREDIENTS | 4 |
| 2.1 THE CHEESE CHRONICLES - A DAIRY TALE | 4 |
| 2.2 THE MEATS TO BEAT - FROM FARM TO FONDUE | 4 |
| 2.3 THE GARDEN GALA - VEGGIE, FRUIT, AND FUNGI FRIENDS | 5 |
| 2.4 THE ALCOHOLIC ART - BALANCING ACT IN A POT | 5 |
| 2.5 THE SWEET SPOT - DAWN OF THE DESSERT FONDUE | 6 |
| CHAPTER 3: FAUX PAS FONDUE - COMMON FONDUE MISHAPS | 6 |
| CHAPTER 4: "SWEET DIPS & DELICIOUS WHIMS - A DESSERT FONDUE FIESTA" | 8 |
| 4.1. NON-ALCOHOLIC WONDERS | 8 |
| 4.1.1.  Recipe 1: "Honeyed Hazelnut Haven" | 8 |
| 4.1.2. Recipe 2: "Minty Mirth Mélange" | 9 |
| 4.1.3. Recipe 3: "Peanut Butter Cup Euphoria" | 9 |
| 4.1.4. Recipe 4: "Salted Caramel Mocha Dip" | 10 |
| 4.1.5. Recipe 5: "Spiced Dark Delight" | 11 |
| 4.1.6. Recipe 6: "Luscious Lemon Cheesecake Dip" | 12 |
| 4.1.7. Recipe 7: "Espresso Your Love Fondue" | 13 |
| 4.1.8. Recipe 8: "S'mores Galore Fondue" | 13 |
| 4.1.9. Recipe 9: "Berry Bliss Redux" | 14 |
| 4.1.10. Recipe 10: "Matcha Maven Meltdown" | 15 |
| 4.1.11. Recipe 11: "Turmeric Twilight Tango" | 16 |
| 4.1.12. Recipe 12: "Sesame Ginger Serenade" | 17 |
| 4.2. SPIRITED SPLENDORS WITH LIQUEURS | 17 |
| 4.2.1.  Recipe 13: "Choco-Cabernet Swirl" | 18 |
| 4.2.2. Recipe 14: "Bourbon Bliss Chocolate Fondue" | 18 |
| 4.2.3. Recipe 15: "Silky Amaretto Ambrosia" | 19 |
| 4.2.4. Recipe 16: "Caramel Apple Rendezvous" | 20 |
| 4.2.5.  Recipe 17: "Velvet Raspberry Truffle Dip" | 21 |
| 4.2.6. Recipe 18: "Toasted Coconut Dream" | 21 |
| 4.2.7. Recipe 19: "Rum Rhapsody Indulgence" | 22 |
| 4.2.8. Recipe 20: "Wild Berry Flambe Fondue" | 23 |
| 4.3. CHILLED DELIGHTS: ICE CREAM FONDUE FANTASIA | 24 |
| 4.3.1. Recipe 21: "Chilled Cream Cascade" | 24 |
| 4.3.2. Recipe 22: "Frozen Fudge Frenzy" | 25 |
| 4.4. A WORLD OF FLAVOR | 26 |
| 4.4.1. Recipe 23: "Samurai's Sweet Retreat" | 26 |

4.4.2. Recipe 24: "Hawaiian Luau Luxe" — 27

4.4.3. Recipe 25: "Amaretto Di Saronno Serenade" — 28

4.4.4. Recipe 26: "Cognac au Chocolat Crémeux" — 29

**CHAPTER 5: "MEAT MORSELS AND SIZZLING SOIREÉS"** — **30**

5.1 "THE FONDUE BOURGUIGNONNE BALLAD" — 30

5.1.1. Recipe 27: "Sirloin Sizzle Soirée" — 30

5.1.2. Recipe 28: "Peppered Filet Fondue Fantasy" — 31

5.1.3. Recipe 29: "Garlic Herb Surf and Turf Plunge" — 32

5.2 "BROTH FONDUE ODYSSEY" — 34

5.2.1. Recipe 30: "Garden Herb Broth Bonanza" — 34

5.2.2. Recipe 31: "Asian Infusion Elixir" — 35

5.2.3. Recipe 32: "Mediterranean Meld Pot" — 36

5.3. "CHINOISERIE CHIC – THE ASIAN HOT POT EXPEDITION" — 37

5.3.1. Recipe 33: "1001 Eastern Nights Hot Pot" — 37

5.3.2. Recipe 34: "Aladdin's Aromatic Adventure" — 38

5.3.3. Recipe 35: "Pharaoh's Feast Broth Pot" — 40

5.4. "POULTRY PLAYHOUSE" — 41

5.4.1. Recipe 36: "Tuscan Chicken Brodo Dip" — 41

5.4.2. Recipe 37: "Lemongrass Coq au Ginger Plunge" — 42

5.4.3. Recipe 38: "Herb-Infused Turkey Temptation" — 43

5.5. "GAME DAY - EXOTIC MEATS AND NOVEL TREATS" — 44

5.5.1. Recipe 39: "Savannah Venison Sizzle" — 45

5.5.2. Recipe 40: "Bison Broth Fondue Frontier" — 45

5.5.3. Recipe 41: "Outback Ostrich Oasis" — 46

5.6. "SAUTÉ AND SAVOR – THE FONDUE CHINOISE CHRONICLES" — 47

5.6.1. Recipe 42: "East Asian Elegance Broth" — 47

5.6.2. Recipe 43: "Shabu-Shabu Symphony" — 48

5.7. "SURF'S UP! - SEAFOOD AND FONDUE HARMONY" — 49

5.7.1. Recipe 44: "Neptune's Nectar Seafood Pot" — 49

5.7.2. Recipe 45: "Lobster Lagoon Fondue" — 50

5.7.3. Recipe 46: "Giant Crab Gala" — 51

5.7.4. Recipe 47: "Mariner's Mélange Mingle" — 52

5.7.5. Recipe 48: "Ocean Trio Spectacle" — 53

5.8. "DIPPING DELICACIES - SAUCES AND SIDES SUPREMACY" — 54

5.8.1.Recipe 49: "Classic Béarnaise Bliss" — 55

5.8.2. Recipe 50: "Zesty Citrus Ponzu Sauce" — 55

5.8.3. Recipe 51: "Creamy Horseradish Concoction" — 56

**CHAPTER 6: "CHEESE CHRONICLES: DIPPING INTO TRADITION"** — **57**

6.1.Classic Cheese Fondue Foundations — 57

6.1.1. Recipe 52: "Traditional Swiss 'moitié-moitié'" — 58

6.1.2. Recipe 53: "Fondue Savoyarde" — 58

6.1.3. Recipe 54: "Gruyère and Garlic Fondue" — 59

6.1.4. Recipe 55: "Alpine Cheese Delight" — 60

6.1.5. Recipe 56: "Cheddar and Beer Fondue Fusion" — 61

6.1.6. Recipe 57: "Fontina Fonduta with Truffle Oil" — 61

6.1.7. Recipe 58: "Champagne and Swiss Cheese Celebration" — 62

6.2. CHEESE FONDUE AROUND THE WORLD — 63

6.2.1. Recipe 59: "Italian Fonduta with Truffles" — 63

6.2.2. Recipe 60: "Classic British Stilton Pot" — 64

6.2.3. Recipe 61: "Mexican Queso Fundido" — 64

6.2.4. Recipe 62: "Canadian Cheddar Chalet"     65

6.2.5. Recipe 63: "Alsatian Munster Melt"     66

6.2.6. Recipe 64: "Dutch Edam Dream"     66

6.2.7. Recipe 65: "Catalan Cava Fondue"     67

6.2.8. Recipe 66: "Greek Feta Fondue"     68

6.2.9. Recipe 67: "Balkan Kajmak Kettle"     69

6.2.10. Recipe 68: "Polish Smoked Oscypek Dip"     69

6.2.11. Recipe 69: "Carpathian Cauldron"     70

6.2.12. Recipe 70: "Caribbean Jerk Cheese Pot"     71

6.2.13. Recipe 71: "South American Chimichurri Cheese Dip"     71

6.2.14. Recipe 72: "Argentinian Provoleta"     72

6.2.15. Recipe 73: "Mexican Fiesta Fondue"     73

6.2.16. Recipe 74: "Tequila & Lime Queso Fundido"     74

6.2.17. Recipe 75: "Chipotle Chorizo Cheese Dip"     74

6.3. "MODERN MELTS: THE ART OF CHEESY INNOVATION"     75

6.3.1. Recipe 76: "Blue Cheese and Fig Fusion"     76

6.3.2. Recipe 77: "Smoked Gouda Lager Luxe"     76

6.3.3. Recipe 78: "Whiskey Cheddar Caramel Dip"     77

6.3.4. Recipe 79: "Harissa Havarti Harmony"     78

6.3.5. Recipe 80: "Port Poached Pear and Gorgonzola Pot"     79

6.3.6. Recipe 81: "Balsamic Fig and Taleggio Cream"     79

6.3.7. Recipe 82: "Roasted Garlic and Goat Cheese River"     80

6.3.8. Recipe 83: "Pesto Genovese Gush"     81

6.3.9. Recipe 84: "Spicy Kimchi Cheese Cauldron"     81

6.4. FROM MILK TO MELT     82

6.5. DIPPER'S DELIGHT: BEYOND THE BASIC BREAD CUBE     89

6.6. CHEESE, WINE, AND BEYOND: A CONNOISSEUR'S COMPANION     91

6.7. FONDUE PARTY PLANNING: THE PERFECT MELTING POT OF FUN     92

6.8. FONDUE ETIQUETTE: THE CHEESE COMMUNAL COMMANDMENTS     94

6.9. CHEESE FONDUE SAFETY TIPS: MELT WITH CARE     95

CHAPTER 7: "FESTIVE FONDUE: RECIPES FOR CHRISTMAS AND NEW YEAR"     97

7.1. A VERY GRUYÈRE CHRISTMAS     97

7.1.1. Recipe 85: "Midnight Mass Emmental Melt"     97

7.1.2. Recipe 86: "Silent Night, Holy Gruyère Fondue"     98

7.2. THE NEW YEAR'S EVE BUBBLY CHEESE POT     98

7.2.1. Recipe 87: "Champagne Cheddar Cheer"     99

7.2.2. Recipe 88: "Prosecco & Pecorino Pop"     99

7.3. SANTA'S SELECTION: CHEESY TREATS FOR THE FAMILY     100

7.3.1. Recipe 89: "Merry Mozzarella Marvel"     100

7.3.2. Recipe 90: "Jingle Bell Cheddar Pot"     101

7.3.3. Recipe 91: "Frosty's Swiss Wonderland"     102

7.4. YULETIDE TWISTS: GLOBAL FONDUE FUSIONS     102

7.4.1. Recipe 92: "Curry Masala Melt"     102

7.4.2. Recipe 93: "Tuscan Truffle Temptation"     103

7.4.3. Recipe 94: "Poblano Pepper Piñata"     104

7.5. AROUND THE FIRE: OUTDOOR FONDUE GATHERINGS     105

7.5.1. Recipe 95: "Campfire Cheese Cascade"     105

7.6. THE NEW YEAR'S DAY BRUNCH FONDUE     106

7.6.1. Recipe 96: "Morning Mimosa Meltdown"     106

7.6.2. Recipe 97: "Sunrise Chèvre Chaud"     107

| | |
|---|---|
| 7.7. The Leftovers Revival Fondue | 108 |
|     *7.7.1. Recipe 98: "Post-Feast Roast Redux"* | *108* |
|     *7.7.2. Recipe 99: "Holiday Ham and Swiss Swirl"* | *109* |
| 7.8. Pairing and Sharing: Festive Drinks and Fondue | 109 |
| 7.9. Fondue Party Games: Holiday Edition | 111 |
| **CHAPTER 8: "GREEN AND LEAN: VEGETARIAN AND DIETARY FONDUE"** | **113** |
| 8.1. Verdant Vats: Vegetable Broth Fondue | 113 |
|     *8.1.1. Recipe 100: "Garden Harvest Brew"* | *113* |
| 8.2. Fromage sans Fromage: Dairy-Free Delights. The Quest for Non-Dairy Nirvana | 114 |
|     *8.2.1. Recipe 101: "The Avocado Avo-lution Dip"* | *114* |
|     *8.2.2. Recipe 102: "Cashew Cauldron Creaminess"* | *115* |
| 8.3. Slim Sauce: Low-Calorie Fondues | 116 |
|     *8.3.1. Recipe 103: "Featherlight Fromage Feast"* | *116* |
|     *8.3.2. Recipe 104: "Garden Gala Dip"* | *117* |
| 8.4. Gluten-Free Gratification: No Bread, No Problem! | 118 |
|     *8.4.1. Recipe 105: "Gluten-Free Gruyère Glide"* | *118* |
|     *8.4.2. Recipe 106: "Cheesy Chickpea Bonanza"* | *119* |
| 8.5. Protein-Packed Pots: Meatless and Mighty | 120 |
|     *8.5.1. Recipe 107: "Soy and Savor Soirée"* | *120* |
|     *8.5.2. Recipe 108: "Legume Lagoon"* | *121* |
| 8.6. The Organic Oasis: Clean and Conscious | 122 |
|     *8.6.1. Recipe 109: "Earth's Embrace Gruyère Fondue"* | *122* |
|     *8.6.2. Recipe 110: "Whole Earth Herb Havarti"* | *123* |
| 8.7. Flavor Without Fuss: Simple and Sensible Fondue Recipes | 124 |
|     *8.7.1.Recipe 111: "Simply Swiss Serenity"* | *124* |
|     *8.7.2. Recipe 112: "Seductively Simple Spinach Soak"* | *124* |
| 8.8. Festive Fodmap-Friendly Fondues | 125 |
|     *8.8.1. Recipe 113: "Gentle Gourmet's Gouda and Grapes"* | *126* |
|     *8.8.2. Recipe 114: "Fructose-Free Fondue Frolic"* | *126* |
| 8.9.Indulgence Inside the Lines: Allergy-Aware Fondues | 127 |
|     *8.9.1. Recipe 115: "Safe Harbor Swiss-style Fondue"* | *128* |
|     *8.9.2. Recipe 116: "Peaceful Peanut-free Pimento Dip"* | *129* |
| **CHAPTER 9: "TWOSOME TABLEAU: FONDUE FOR TWO"** | **130** |
| 9.1. Let's dive into a romantic fondue experience designed for a cozy night in. | 130 |
|     *9.1.1. Recipe 117:Svelte Alpine Night* | *130* |
|     *9.1.2. Recipe 118:Choco-Berry Whisper* | *131* |
|     *9.1.3. Recipe 119:Tipsy Twosome and Tipsy Cheddar* | *132* |
| 9.2."Candlelit Classics" | 133 |
|     *9.2.1. Recipe 120: "Intimate Emmental and Gruyère Embrace"* | *133* |
|     *9.2.2. Recipe 121: "Chocolate Fondue for Two"* | *134* |
| 9.3. Seduction by Dippers | 135 |
| 9.4. Bubbly and Cheese | 136 |
| 9.5. Melt of the Moment | 137 |
|     *9.5.1. Recipe 122: "Honeyed Blue Cheese Euphoria"* | *138* |
|     *9.5.2. Recipe 123: "Whisper of Smoked Gouda Bliss"* | *138* |
| 9.6. Recipes for Romance | 139 |
|     *9.6.1. Recipe 124: "Ardent Asiago and Artichoke Amore"* | *139* |
|     *9.6.2. Recipe 125: "Brie and Berries Ballet"* | *140* |
| 9.7. Sweets for the Sweet | 141 |
|     *9.7.1. Recipe 126: "Dark Decadence and Fruit Fantasia"* | *141* |

*9.7.2. Recipe 127: "Caramel Cream Dream"*      *142*

**9.8.** LOVE POTIONS AND LIBATIONS      143

**9.9.** NOCTURNE OF NOURISHMENT      144

*9.9.1. Recipe 128: "Hearts Aflame Avocado Fondue"*      *144*

*9.9.2. Recipe 129: "Alpine Essence Edamame Dip"*      *145*

**CHAPTER 10: "THE GRAND FINALE: A FONDUE OVATION"**      **148**

# Chapter 1: A Grande Melt-roduction to Fondue

## 1.1. The Chronicles of Cheese: A Gooey Tale Retold

Let's crank up the wheels of time to when fondue was not just a dish but a survival strategy. Swiss families used to huddle around a communal pot, dipping in old bread to soften it up—talk about a medieval life hack! Allegedly, it was a clever tactic devised by thrifty mountain-dwellers or possibly resourceful monks (who, let's face it, have always had a knack for booze and cheese-related innovations).

Here's a fun fondue fact to nibble on: Fondue became Switzerland's national dish in the 1930s thanks to a big push by—drumroll, please—the Swiss Cheese Union who decided to melt themselves into the hearts and stomachs of the world. Imagine that! It was the tastiest propaganda campaign ever.

As for the big 'fondue party' era of the 1960s, picture this: a jazzy tune on the record player, shag carpets, and that brand-new fondue set from the wedding registry making its debut. It wasn't just dinner; it was a happening, an edible event!

## 1.2. Fondue's Rich Palette – A Dip into Diversity

### Cheese Fondue - The Pot of Liquid Gold

The quintessential cheese fondue is like a warm hug from the inside. The original recipe, revered as "moitié-moitié" (half-half), dances in your mouth with a blend of Gruyère and Fribourg vacherin cheeses. But there's a wild world of cheese out there waiting to be melted. Fondue Savoyarde throws in some Beaufort, while Fonduta uses Fontina and eggs for an Italian twist.

Picture this: it's 1956, and the first televised cooking show in color broadcasts a cheese fondue demo. Viewers almost climb through their screens to get a dip—talk about a historic moment in 'television taste testing'!

### Chocolate Fondue - The Swirl of Sweet Seduction

In need of a romance catalyzer? Enter chocolate fondue. Debuted in New York in the 1960s, it's been warming cold dates ever since. Delightfully gentle on the palate, the chocolate fondue is often a loving mix of dark and milk chocolate with a dash of heavy cream. Indulge in an "à la minute" fondue with exotic fruits or get all-American with brownie bites and marshmallows.

Did you know? Chocolate fondue was actually popularized by a Swiss restaurateur in the Big Apple. It's like the cheese fondue's alter ego, dressed in black and ready to seduce.

1

## Oil or Broth Fondue - The Festive Fryer

We've opened Pandora's pot now—cooking meat in sizzling oil or gently simmering in aromatic broth at the table is quite the visceral experience. Born from a tradition as old as cooking itself, the oil fondue is not for the faint of heart. And yes, there's a chance of an oil-spatter incident of '73—which guests still laugh about at reunions.

In broth fondue, you turn to seasoned stocks as a flavorful hot bath for your meats and veggies. It's healthier, less hazardous, and echoes exotic traditions like the Chinese hot pot, where a shared pot is not just about food; it's about fortune and family.

### *The A-Z of Alternative Fondue Adventures*

Adventurous souls have wandered off the beaten cheese path into pots of bubbling tomato sauce, creamy garlic, or even spiced curry for dunking meats and bread. The creativity in fondue knows no bounds—and neither do the post-fondue naps.

# 1.3. The Fondue Kit Chronicles - Tools of the Dip Trade

## The Fondue Pot - Not Just Another Pot on the Shelf

A ceramic pot is like the Fondue world's cozy sweater, perfect for the gooey glide of cheese and the tender clasp of chocolate. Then there's the cast iron or stainless-steel pot, a knight in shining armor for the high-heat jousting of oil or broth fondue.

## The Heat Beneath - The Burner Saga

Burners have stories too—like the time someone forgot to refill the fuel and the flame went out mid-party. There's a gel and alcohol-based fuel for a classic touch, or you can find an electric burner that promises a flame-free, no-refill experience—spicy!

## Fondue Forks - The Swords of Social Snacking

Equipped with color-coded handles to wave off any double-dipping suspicions, fondue forks are not for the shy eater. They are, in fact, your trusty allies in the quest for that piece of bread you lost in the cheese abyss.

## The Circuit of Add-ons - The Accoutrements Alliance

From bread baskets to dipping trays and condiment bowls—each fondue accessory has a role. And don't forget about the splash guards and the unsung heroes of smooth fondue affairs—the pot holders, lest you handle the hot pot and become the evening's hottest topic!

Stick with me, the maestro of melty goodness, and you'll learn to navigate the bubbly, sizzling, and chocolate-drenched seas of fondue etiquette, adventure, and delight. Prepare to dip into the gourmet galaxy of fondue—your pot awaits!

And there you have it, our first dive into the delicious, delightful world of fondue. Next chapters will expertly skewer everything from traditional recipes to contemporary twists, ensuring your fondue nights are forever etched in the annals of culinary legend. Stay tuned, dip dreamers!

## 1.4. "The Fondue Safety Dance"

As with every great performance, safety is key. This final note ensures you cook at the right temperatures, avoid the taboo of double-dipping with raw meats, and keep your fondue soirée a deliciously safe affair. Absolutely, safety is paramount when it comes to enjoying fondue, especially those involving hot oils and broths. Here are some key safety tips to consider:

**Fondue Safety Tips:**

1. Stable Heat Source: Ensure your fondue set has a stable heat source and is placed on a steady, heat-resistant surface. Never leave it unattended while it's hot.
2. Appropriate Fuel: Use only the fuel recommended by your fondue pot's manufacturer, and never overfill the burner. Keep spare fuel away from the lit fondue pot to avoid any accidental flare-ups.
3. Correct Cooking Temperatures: Maintain the oil or broth at the recommended temperatures for cooking (usually around 350°F to 375°F for oil, and simmering gently for broth). Use a thermometer to monitor and ensure meats are cooked to safe internal temperatures.
4. No Cross-Contamination: Raw meats should be handled with care. Use separate platters for raw and cooked meats and ensure cooking utensils don't cross-contaminate.
5. Fondue Fork Safety: Fondue forks are sharp and can get very hot. Use them only for cooking and transferring food from the pot to your plate, not for eating. Provide guests with separate dining forks or plates to avoid accidental burns.
6. Handling Hot Oil or Broth: Be cautious when dipping into hot oil or broth to prevent splatters. Move slowly and gently place food into the pot without letting go of it until it's submerged.
7. Supervise Children: If children are present, adult supervision is crucial at all times. Teach them the importance of moving slowly around the fondue set and the proper use of skewers.
8. Preventing Overcrowding: Don't overcrowd the pot as it will lower the temperature of the oil or broth and can lead to uneven cooking.
9. Managing Spills: In case of oil or broth spills, immediately turn off the heat source if it is safe to do so and move everyone away from the area. Use baking soda to help extinguish oil fires, not water.
10. Serving Hot: Remember that the fondue pot, especially metal ones used for frying, can be extremely hot. Warn guests not to touch the pot during the meal.

By following these safety steps, hosts and guests alike can relish the fondue experience while keeping the fun uninterrupted by unwanted accidents. With vigilant care, your fondue party will be remembered for the lively conversations and delicious food, not for mishaps!

# Chapter 2: The Fondue-volution of Ingredients

Welcome back, fondue aficionados and cheese whisperers! Grab your forks and notebooks because, in this encyclopedia of edibles, we're diving into the very essence of fondue perfection—the ingredients. Get ready to become a procurement prodigy for all your fondue fantasies!

## 2.1 The Cheese Chronicles - A Dairy Tale

### The Swiss Symphony

In the cheese corner, we have the Swiss superstars—Gruyère and Emmental. Gruyère, the Sean Connery of cheeses, brings a nutty and slightly sweet sophistication to your pot. Emmental, with its holes and mild flavor, plays the supporting role like a trusty sidekick.

### The French Connection

From the Land of Love and Baguettes come Comté with its fruity notes and Beaufort with a buttery finish. Dip into a Fondue Savoyarde by blending these enfants together for a tres magnifique melange.

### The Italian Incanto

Seeking an Italian opera in a pot? Enter Fontina with its earthy whisper and Taleggio with a tangy nudge, melting into a Fonduta that hugs your bread like Nonna's embrace.

### The Intrepid International

Want a global cheeseboard experience? Consider tangy Cheddar, smoky Gouda, or creamy Brie. Picture the time someone accidentally dropped blue cheese into the pot, and the result was a surprisingly delicious "bleu" moon event.

## 2.2 The Meats to Beat - From Farm to Fondue

### Beefing it Up

Select cuts like sirloin or filet mignon sizzle in the pot, turning your dinner into an interactive steakhouse experience. Remember the great meatball mishap of '87? They weren't thin enough, and we dined at midnight!

### The Poultry Club

Chicken and turkey tenderloins, when deftly sliced, swim elegantly through oil or broth, reminding us of the 'Great Chicken Dance Off' at Aunt Sally's fondue fiesta.

### The Swimmers

Seafood like shrimp, scallops, or thin slices of salmon elevate your fondue to mythical Neptune's feast levels. There's always that one dude who thought "sushi-style" in the broth pot was a good idea—spoiler: it wasn't.

### The Oddballs

Remember the time someone dunked venison into the pot, and it was a game-changer or experimented with tofu, and the vegetarians rejoiced? Fondue is the edible Wild West—no meat is off-limits (within reason).

## 2.3 The Garden Gala - Veggie, Fruit, and Fungi Friends

### The Veggie Patch

Broccoli, carrots, and bell peppers don't just bring the crunch; they bring the color. Let's take a moment to honor the green bean that sacrificed itself to the fondue gods for the perfect dip.

### Orchard Offerings

Apples and pears, with their crisp sweetness, battle the cheese's richness. And let's not forget the grapes that caused a "grape laughter" outbreak due to their slippery escape attempts.

### Mushroom Medley

Whether it's the classic button or the exotic Shiitake, mushrooms have sashayed their way into the hearts of fondue pots everywhere. There's a fabled tale about a wild truffle fondue adventure, but that's for the gourmet gossip column.

## 2.4 The Alcoholic Art - Balancing Act in a Pot

### The White Wines

Dry white wines like a snappy Sauvignon Blanc or a lively Chardonnay are not just cooking ingredients; they're conversation starters. Remember that time Uncle Bob flambéed his eyebrows adding wine to the flame? Classic!

### The Spirits

Kirsch, the cherry spirit, may not turn your fondue into a fruit bowl, but it sure does ignite the flavor (and the pot if you're not careful—RIP Aunt Edna's tablecloth).

### Drinking Buddies

Thinking of a booze pairing? A crisp white wine, a light beer, or even a cup of steaming tea can be your pot's best buddy, preventing the notorious "fondue coma."

## 2.5 The Sweet Spot - Dawn of the Dessert Fondue

### Chocolate Galore

Mix your favorite—dark, milk, or white chocolates—and remember that time someone tried to fondue with chocolate chips and created a lumpy chocolate mountain.

### Cream and Dreams

Heavy cream is the river upon which your chocolate boat sails. That one Thanksgiving? When someone used milk instead? Let's just say it was more of a canoe trip.

### Sweet Accents

Think outside the chocolate box. Add a touch of cinnamon, a splash of vanilla, or even a peppermint twist for a holiday surprise—like the time the fondue turned pink on Valentine's Day.

### Fruit Fountains and Beyond

Skewer those strawberries, bananas, and pineapples; after all, the fruit kabob incident of '92 showed us that presentation makes the party.

This concludes our second chapter, where the ingredients are not just sustenance; they're the stars, the drama, and the punchline of every fondue story. As you stock your pantry and prepare your mise en place, get ready to create your unique tales of fondue wonder. What will your next fondue soirée bring? A thriller, a rom-com, or perhaps an epic culinary saga! Stay tuned for the recipe roundup, where we blend tradition with innovation in an awe-inspiring fondue festival for your taste buds. Keep those forks ready, chefs—it's going to be a bountiful dip.

# Chapter 3: Faux Pas Fondue - Common Fondue Mishaps

### The Great Cheese Seizure

The number one blunder in the fondue world? Rushing the cheese! The key to creamy goodness is patience. Turn up the heat too high, too fast, and you'll end up with a grainy, separated disaster worthy of a cheese horror film.

### Wine Woes

Adding wine all at once is like flooding a dance floor before anyone can two-step. The trick is a slow drizzle, a little at a time, to let the cheese and wine fall madly in love at their own pace.

## Bread Bloopers

Stale bread is a must—but not so stale it could double as a hockey puck. And remember to cube, not crumble; unless you like fishing for breadcrumbs in a sea of cheese.

## Boiling Point Panic

A rolling boil in the oil pot? Unless you're aiming for Fondue Volcano, with splattering oil and cooked-on-the-outside, raw-on-the-inside meats, keep it at a simmer, my friends.

## Fruit Faux Pas

Juicy fruits like watermelon in a cheese fondue - a delicious mistake waiting to happen. The excess water can turn that pot into a muddled mess. Stick to the firmer fruits that know how to handle a cheese dip.

## The Double Dip Debacle

Fondue is delicious, yes, but manners, please! Double-dipping is not just a party foul; it's a fondue felony. Forks out after one dip!

## Skimping on Skewers

You can't skimp on fondue forks. Regular forks just don't have the reach. Unless you're fond of scorching your fingertips – invest in the correct equipment.

## Chunky Chocolate Chaos

Chocolate Fondue gone grainy? That's likely from a choco-cheese melt method mix-up. Keep water away, and heat gently for a satin-smooth sweet retreat.

## The Wrong Pot Plot

A basic pot mistake that can spoil the lot. You wouldn't brew tea in a colander, so use the right pot—ceramic pots for cheese and chocolate; metal for oil and broth.

## Condiment Confusion

Last but not least, overdoing condiments is like a comedian with a bad punchline—it can ruin a great setup. Complement, don't overpower, and let the fondue be the star of your show.

Remember, folks, fondue is as much about the journey as it is about the destination. Avoid these snags, and you'll be sailing smooth on fondue seas. IsPlainOldData

# Chapter 4: "Sweet Dips & Delicious Whims - A Dessert Fondue Fiesta"

Welcome to a chapter where every page drips with sweet indulgence—where you'll discover an array of dessert fondues that tantalize, comfort, and celebrate. Whether you're seeking a nightcap without the cap or an indulgence that tempts the palate with intoxicating spirits, our carefully curated sections are tailored just for you. And for those fondue pilgrims that chase the setting sun, we have national recipes that bring the flavors of the world to your pot. Here's a whimsically sweet fondue recipe to start your chapter on dessert fondue festivities.

## 4.1. Non-Alcoholic Wonders

### 4.1.1. Recipe 1: "Honeyed Hazelnut Haven"

Yield: 4 servings | Preparation time: 10 minutes | Cooking time: 8 minutes.

Ingredients:

- 1/2 cup Nutella or chocolate-hazelnut spread
- 1/4 cup honey
- 1/2 cup heavy cream
- 1/4 teaspoon ground cinnamon
- Assorted dippers: banana slices, strawberries, biscotti, and marshmallows

Directions:

1. Over low heat, whisk together the chocolate-hazelnut spread, honey, and heavy cream in a small saucepan until the mixture is evenly combined and warm.
2. Add a dash of cinnamon to the mix, stirring for a subtle spicy note.
3. Transfer the warm, nutty concoction to a fondue pot, keeping the flame low to maintain a dip-worthy consistency.
4. Circle the pot with your chosen dippers, from fresh fruit to toasty biscotti, ready for the dipping delight.

Nutrition information:

Nutritional value: Approximately 460 calories, 4g protein, 53g carbohydrates, 28g fats, 2g fiber, 20mg cholesterol, 35mg sodium, 250mg potassium per serving.

---

Savor this dip of decadence where hazelnut and honey unite for a sweet symphony, enchanting your evening and seducing your spread.

### 4.1.2. Recipe 2: "Minty Mirth Mélange"

Yield: 4 servings | Preparation time: 10 minutes | Cooking time: 5 minutes.

Ingredients:

- 8 ounces white chocolate, chopped
- 1/3 cup heavy cream
- 2 tablespoons crème de menthe
- 1 tablespoon unsalted butter
- Chocolate cookies, brownie chunks, fresh pineapple, and kiwi slices for dipping

Directions:

1. In a saucepan over low heat, combine the heavy cream and butter, stirring until the butter is melted and the cream is hot to the touch.
2. Gradually add the white chocolate to the cream, constantly stirring until completely melted and silky smooth.
3. Stir in the crème de menthe, lending a refreshing minty twist to the fondue.
4. Transfer to a fondue pot set over a low flame to keep warm without losing that velvety texture.
5. Serve with an assortment of chocolate cookies, brownie chunks, pineapple, and kiwi, creating a playful contrast of flavors.

Nutrition information:

Nutritional value: Approximately 520 calories, 4g protein, 50g carbohydrates, 34g fats, 1g fiber, 25mg cholesterol, 80mg sodium, 220mg potassium per serving.

---

This concoction brings a burst of cool mint and creamy chocolate to your dessert spread, making for an irresistibly refreshing fondue adventure.

### 4.1.3. Recipe 3: "Peanut Butter Cup Euphoria"

Yield: 6 servings | Preparation time: 5 minutes | Cooking time: 10 minutes.

Ingredients:

- 1 cup smooth peanut butter
- 2/3 cup heavy cream
- 6 ounces semisweet chocolate, chopped

- 1 tablespoon honey
- Pinch of salt
- Assorted dippers: pretzel rods, apple slices, marshmallows, and graham crackers

Directions:

1. In a saucepan over low heat, warm the heavy cream until it begins to steam. Be cautious not to allow it to boil.
2. Slowly whisk in the peanut butter, chocolate, honey, and a pinch of salt, stirring consistently until the mixture is smoothly combined and the chocolate has fully melted.
3. Transfer the fondue to a fondue pot, maintaining a gentle heat to ensure the fondue stays warm and liquid.
4. Arrange your preferred dippers around the fondue pot, offering a delightful mix of sweet and salty treats for your indulgence.

Nutrition information:

Nutritional value: Approximately 515 calories, 12g protein, 30g carbohydrates, 40g fats, 4g fiber, 20mg cholesterol, 250mg sodium, 370mg potassium per serving.

---

Prepare for your taste buds to be coated in the glory of peanut butter and chocolate—a duo that has danced in harmony since the dawn of candy time. This fondue recipe captures the thrill of unwrapping peanut butter cups, transformed into a shareable pot of joy.

## 4.1.4. Recipe 4: "Salted Caramel Mocha Dip"

Yield: 4 servings | Preparation time: 5 minutes | Cooking time: 7 minutes.

Ingredients:

- 1 cup caramel pieces or caramel sauce
- 1/2 cup heavy cream
- 4 ounces dark chocolate, chopped
- 1 tablespoon instant espresso powder
- A pinch of flaky sea salt (plus more for garnish)
- Assorted dippers: brownie chunks, vanilla wafer cookies, strawberries, and marshmallows

Directions:

1. Gently heat caramel and heavy cream in a saucepan over low heat, stirring until the caramel is melted and the mixture is smooth.
2. Add the chopped dark chocolate and espresso powder, stirring constantly until the chocolate is melted and the fondue has a consistent mocha color.
3. Once fully combined, transfer the fondue to a pot set over a low flame. Sprinkle with a pinch of flaky sea salt for a subtle contrast.
4. Garnish the edge of the serving platter with a sprinkle of sea salt. Serve with an assortment of dippers for that perfect sweet and salty flavor combination.

Nutrition information:

Nutritional value: Approximately 520 calories, 4g protein, 65g carbohydrates, 29g fats, 3g fiber, 30mg cholesterol, 230mg sodium, 210mg potassium per serving.

---

The salted caramel and mocha elements of this fondue create a harmonious ballet of bold and comforting flavors, a sweet symphony for the daring dessert lover. It's a gourmet twist that nods to the cozy corners of your favorite coffee shop enveloped in caramel warmth.

## 4.1.5. Recipe 5: "Spiced Dark Delight"

Yield: 4 servings | Preparation time: 15 minutes | Cooking time: 8 minutes.

Ingredients:

- 8 ounces high-quality dark chocolate (70% cacao), coarsely chopped
- 2/3 cup heavy cream
- 1 teaspoon ground cinnamon
- 1/4 teaspoon ground nutmeg
- 1/4 teaspoon cayenne pepper
- Assorted dippers: crystallized ginger, orange segments, raspberries, and chunks of angel food cake

Directions:

1. Heat heavy cream in a saucepan over medium-low heat until warm, then stir in the cinnamon, nutmeg, and cayenne pepper.
2. Add the dark chocolate to the pan and whisk until fully melted and the spices are well blended into the mixture.
3. Carefully pour the chocolate blend into your fondue pot and keep it warm with a low flame.
4. Arrange your chosen dippers on all sides for a warming, chocolate-spiced adventure.

Nutrition information:

Nutritional value: Approximately 490 calories, 5g protein, 45g carbohydrates, 35g fats, 7g fiber, 25mg cholesterol, 20mg sodium, 460mg potassium per serving.

---

The "Spiced Dark Delight" is a sensory escapade, with a blend of spices kicking the smooth dark chocolate up a notch, proving that sometimes, a little spice is indeed everything nice in the land of chocolate fondue.

## 4.1.6. Recipe 6: "Luscious Lemon Cheesecake Dip"

Yield: 4 servings | Preparation time: 10 minutes | Cooking time: 10 minutes.

Ingredients:

- 8 ounces cream cheese, softened
- 1/2 cup sour cream
- 1/4 cup granulated sugar
- 2 tablespoons lemon zest
- 3 tablespoons fresh lemon juice
- Assorted dippers: graham crackers, blueberries, shortbread cookies, and pound cake cubes

Directions:

1. In a medium saucepan over low heat, whisk together the cream cheese, sour cream, and sugar until the mixture is smooth and sugar has dissolved.
2. Stir in the lemon zest and lemon juice until the mixture is creamy and citrus-infused.
3. Transfer the lemon cheesecake mixture into a fondue pot set over a low flame to keep it temptingly warm and smooth.
4. Serve with a delightful medley of graham crackers, plump blueberries, shortbread cookies, and pound cake cubes for dipping.

Nutrition information:

Nutritional value: Approximately 425 calories, 6g protein, 40g carbohydrates, 28g fats, 0g fiber, 90mg cholesterol, 220mg sodium, 160mg potassium per serving.

---

Prepare your palate for a zesty journey where the tangy thrill of lemon swirls with the creamy, dreamy cheesecake base in a fondue pot—every dip whispers 'dessert without the formality'.

### 4.1.7. Recipe 7: "Espresso Your Love Fondue"

Yield: 4 servings | Preparation time: 10 minutes | Cooking time: 5 minutes.

Ingredients:

- 8 ounces bittersweet chocolate, chopped
- 1/2 cup half-and-half
- 2 tablespoons freshly brewed espresso
- 1 teaspoon pure vanilla extract
- A pinch of fine sea salt
- Assorted dippers: biscotti, ladyfingers, sliced strawberries, and marshmallows

Directions:

1. Heat half-and-half in a saucepan over medium-low until it begins to steam, then reduce heat to low.
2. Stir in the chopped chocolate and continue stirring until fully melted and incorporated with the cream.
3. Add the freshly brewed espresso, vanilla extract, and a pinch of sea salt, stirring until the mixture is smooth and fragrant.
4. Pour the mixture into a fondue pot set over a low flame to keep the fondue warm and velvety.
5. Arrange a selection of biscotti, ladyfingers, strawberries, and marshmallows around the pot for guests to dip and enjoy.

Nutrition information:

Nutritional value: Approximately 490 calories, 4g protein, 45g carbohydrates, 32g fats, 5g fiber, 15mg cholesterol, 130mg sodium, 370mg potassium per serving.

---

This fondue is a romantic ode to coffee lovers and chocolate enthusiasts alike, creating a perfect union that's sure to stir the heart and tantalize the taste buds. Indulge in the depth of espresso and the richness of chocolate in one smooth dip.

### 4.1.8. Recipe 8: "S'mores Galore Fondue"

Yield: 4 servings | Preparation time: 5 minutes | Cooking time: 5 minutes.

Ingredients:

- 8 ounces milk chocolate, roughly chopped
- 1/2 cup heavy cream
- 1/4 cup marshmallow fluff

- 1/4 teaspoon cinnamon
- Graham crackers and additional marshmallows for dipping

Directions:

1. Combine the chocolate and heavy cream in a saucepan over low heat, stirring until the chocolate is completely melted and the mixture is smooth.
2. Stir in the marshmallow fluff and cinnamon until everything is well-blended and heated through.
3. Pour the mixture into a fondue pot or serve directly from the saucepan if a fondue pot is not available.
4. Break the graham crackers into dip-sized pieces, and if feeling extra indulgent, toast the extra marshmallows before serving alongside for a delightful dip.

Nutrition information:

Nutritional value: Approximately 420 calories, 3g protein, 45g carbohydrates, 25g fats, 2g fiber, 24mg cholesterol, 60mg sodium, 210mg potassium per serving.

---

This "S'mores Galore Fondue" is perfect for teens or anyone looking for a quick and joyful dip into childhood memories. Simple and fun, it's perfect for sleepovers, movie nights, or any gathering that needs a touch of sweet, gooey goodness. No campfire is needed!

## 4.1.9. Recipe 9: "Berry Bliss Redux"

Yield: 4 servings | Preparation time: 10 minutes | Cooking time: 6 minutes.

Ingredients:

- 8 ounces white chocolate, finely chopped
- 1/3 cup heavy cream
- 2 tablespoons mixed berry preserves
- 1 teaspoon orange zest
- Fresh berries (strawberries, blueberries, raspberries), angel food cake cubes, and ladyfingers for dipping

Directions:

1. Warm the heavy cream over low heat in a saucepan until it begins to steam, then whisk in the white chocolate until completely melted and smooth.
2. Mix in the berry preserves and orange zest, stirring until the fondue is fragrantly fruity and well combined.

3. Transfer the fondue to a serving pot, keeping the flame low to maintain its smooth texture.
4. Provide an array of fresh berries, angel food cake cubes, and ladyfingers for an irresistible treat that's a visual feast as much as a taste sensation.

Nutrition information:

Nutritional value: Approximately 405 calories, 4g protein, 49g carbohydrates, 22g fats, 1g fiber, 20mg cholesterol, 35mg sodium, 190mg potassium per serving.

---

Indulge in a fondue that hints at the freshness of a summer berry patch with an added zesty orange twist. It's a light yet luxurious dessert that marries the elegance of white chocolate with the tart sweetness of berry preserves—inspired by lazy afternoons and garden delights.

## 4.1.10. Recipe 10: "Matcha Maven Meltdown"

Yield: 4 servings | Preparation time: 10 minutes | Cooking time: 5 minutes.

Ingredients:

- 8 ounces white chocolate, chopped
- 1/2 cup heavy cream
- 2 teaspoons matcha green tea powder
- 1 tablespoon honey
- Fresh fruit slices like peaches and pears, mochi pieces, and wafer cookies for dipping

Directions:

1. Over low heat, whisk together the heavy cream and matcha powder in a saucepan until the matcha is fully dissolved and the mixture is an even, vibrant green.
2. Add the honey, then slowly incorporate the white chocolate, stirring continuously until melted and the mixture is smooth.
3. Once fully combined, transfer the matcha-infused fondue to a pot kept warm over a low flame.
4. Serve this avant-garde fondue with slices of fresh fruit, soft mochi, and crisp wafer cookies for a contemporary take on the traditional dessert fondue.

Nutrition information:

Nutritional value: Approximately 420 calories, 3g protein, 35g carbohydrates, 29g fats, 1g fiber, 30mg cholesterol, 40mg sodium, 120mg potassium per serving.

Embrace the zen of dipping with this "Matcha Maven Meltdown"—a nod to the serene and health-conscious trends of the last few years. The delicate, earthy flavor of matcha blends beautifully with sweet white chocolate, creating a modern fusion that's as sophisticated as it is sensational.

### 4.1.11. Recipe 11: "Turmeric Twilight Tango"

Yield: 4 servings | Preparation time: 10 minutes | Cooking time: 5 minutes.

Ingredients:

- 8 ounces milk chocolate, chopped
- 1/2 cup coconut milk
- 1 teaspoon turmeric powder
- 1/4 teaspoon ground cinnamon
- A pinch of black pepper
- 2 tablespoons maple syrup
- Assorted dippers: pineapple chunks, apple slices, marshmallows, and banana bread pieces

Directions:

1. In a saucepan, stir together the coconut milk, turmeric, cinnamon, and black pepper over low heat until the spices are well-blended and the mixture is warm. The pepper enhances turmeric's bioavailability, making this a health-conscious choice.
2. Add the milk chocolate to the pan and continue to stir as it melts into the spiced coconut milk. Stir in the maple syrup for a touch of natural sweetness.
3. Once the chocolate is totally melted and the fondue is uniform, transfer it to your fondue pot set over a gentle flame to keep it warm.
4. Prepare a platter of exotic and traditional dippers like fresh pineapple, crisp apple slices, spongy marshmallows, and hearty banana bread for dipping.

Nutrition information:

Nutritional value: Approximately 360 calories, 3g protein, 44g carbohydrates, 20g fats, 2g fiber, 10mg cholesterol, 25mg sodium, 300mg potassium per serving.

---

"Turmeric Twilight Tango" invites you to a dance of flavors where ancient spices meet modern indulgence in a milk chocolate fondue setting. Each dip is an opportunity to explore a sensational blend of sweetness, spice, and everything nice.

### 4.1.12. Recipe 12: "Sesame Ginger Serenade"

Yield: 4 servings | Preparation time: 15 minutes | Cooking time: 10 minutes.

Ingredients:

- 8 ounces white chocolate, finely chopped
- 1/3 cup heavy cream
- 2 teaspoons toasted sesame oil
- 1 tablespoon finely grated fresh ginger
- 1 teaspoon sesame seeds, toasted
- Assorted dippers: mandarin orange segments, lychee fruits, pound cake cubes, and almond cookies

Directions:

1. Warm the heavy cream in a saucepan on low heat until it begins to steam. Stir in the grated ginger and toasted sesame oil, infusing the cream with their aromatic essence.
2. Gradually add the white chocolate to the spiced cream mixture, stirring until the chocolate is melted and the fondue is silken and smooth.
3. Sprinkle in the toasted sesame seeds and give the mixture one final gentle stir.
4. Transfer the uniquely flavored fondue to a pot with a low flame, keeping it at the perfect temperature for dipping.
5. Serve with an array of dippers that complement the fondue's oriental flair, like sweet mandarin oranges, juicy lychee, spongy pound cake, and crisp almond cookies.

Nutrition information:

Nutritional value: Approximately 390 calories, 3g protein, 35g carbohydrates, 27g fats, 1g fiber, 25mg cholesterol, 40mg sodium, 150mg potassium per serving.

---

The "Sesame Ginger Serenade" fondue is a harmonious melody of East meets West. It's a dessert that invites adventurous palates to explore the delicate dance of sweet white chocolate with the nutty depth of sesame and the warm, spicy notes of ginger.

## 4.2. Spirited Splendors with Liqueurs

For the connoisseurs who find joy in the melding of liqueurs and chocolate, this section is an ode to fondue with a touch of gaiety. Here, each recipe is a delight, each dip an encounter with a spirited chocolate concoction that's playful and bold.

## 4.2.1. Recipe 13: "Choco-Cabernet Swirl"

Yield: 4 servings | Preparation time: 15 minutes | Cooking time: 10 minutes.

Ingredients:

- 8 ounces high-quality semisweet chocolate, chopped
- 1/2 cup full-bodied Cabernet Sauvignon
- 1/4 cup heavy cream
- 2 tablespoons honey
- 1/2 teaspoon pure vanilla extract
- A pinch of sea salt
- Assorted dippers: strawberries, sliced bananas, marshmallows, angel food cake cubes, and pretzel sticks

Directions:

1. Combine the chocolate, Cabernet Sauvignon, and heavy cream in a medium, heavy-bottomed saucepan. Over low heat, melt the ingredients together, stirring constantly until smooth and homogenous.
2. Stir in the honey, vanilla extract, and a pinch of sea salt, continuing to cook for an additional minute or until the mixture is glossy and all ingredients are well-incorporated.
3. Transfer the fondue to a fondue pot set over a low flame to keep warm. Arrange an assortment of dippers on a platter around the fondue pot.
4. Invite guests to skewer their choice of dippers and swirl them into the chocolate wine fondue, letting each bite be an exploration of rich, decadent flavor.

    Nutrition information:

Nutritional value: Approximately 510 calories, 5g protein, 50g carbohydrates, 30g fats, 3g fiber, 15mg cholesterol, 120mg sodium, 400mg potassium per serving.

## 4.2.2. Recipe 14: "Bourbon Bliss Chocolate Fondue"

Yield: 4 servings | Preparation time: 10 minutes | Cooking time: 8 minutes.

Ingredients:

- 8 ounces milk chocolate, finely chopped
- 3 tablespoons smooth bourbon
- 1/2 cup heavy whipping cream
- 1 teaspoon light brown sugar
- 1/4 teaspoon ground cinnamon

- Marshmallows, pound cake cubes, apple slices, and wafer cookies for dipping

Directions:

1. In a medium saucepan, whisk together the heavy cream, bourbon, brown sugar, and cinnamon over medium-low heat until the sugar is dissolved and the mixture is warm (not boiling).
2. Remove from heat and add the chopped milk chocolate, stirring until the chocolate is completely melted and the fondue is smooth.
3. Pour the chocolate bourbon mixture into a fondue pot set over a gentle flame to keep the fondue warm and inviting.
4. Serve with an assortment of marshmallows, pound cake cubes, apple slices, and wafer cookies for a party-pleasing array of textures and flavors.

Nutrition information:

Nutritional value: Approximately 525 calories, 4g protein, 52g carbohydrates, 32g fats, 2g fiber, 20mg cholesterol, 85mg sodium, 300mg potassium per serving.

---

This recipe brings a touch of Southern charm to your dessert table, combining the richness of chocolate with the warmth of bourbon. Enjoy these sweet moments of indulgence, and ready your forks for the next recipe!

## 4.2.3. Recipe 15: "Silky Amaretto Ambrosia"

Yield: 4 servings | Preparation time: 10 minutes | Cooking time: 5 minutes.

Ingredients:

- 8 ounces white chocolate, chopped
- 1/2 cup heavy cream
- 1/4 cup amaretto liqueur
- 1/2 teaspoon almond extract
- Assorted dippers: fresh figs, apricots, biscotti, and almond biscotti

Directions:

1. Combine the white chocolate and heavy cream in a saucepan. Gently heat over low, stirring frequently, until the chocolate has fully melted and integrated with the cream.
2. Stir in the amaretto liqueur and almond extract, mixing thoroughly until the fondue is smooth and emits a heavenly scent.

3. Transfer to a fondue pot, keeping the flame low to maintain the fondue's luxurious consistency.
4. Present with a platter of fresh figs, apricots, and almond biscotti for a divine dipping experience.

Nutrition information:

Nutritional value: Approximately 490 calories, 4g protein, 45g carbohydrates, 28g fats, 1g fiber, 25mg cholesterol, 70mg sodium, 210mg potassium per serving.

---

Elevate your taste buds to the clouds with this angelic blend of white chocolate and amaretto. Dip, bite, and savor each morsel in this luscious liquid treasure.

## 4.2.4. Recipe 16: "Caramel Apple Rendezvous"

Yield: 6 servings | Preparation time: 15 minutes | Cooking time: 10 minutes.

Ingredients:

- 1 cup caramel sauce
- 2 tablespoons calvados (apple brandy)
- 1/2 teaspoon sea salt
- 1/4 teaspoon ground cinnamon
- Assorted dippers: apple slices, pear slices, salted pretzels, and pound cake cubes

Directions:

1. In a medium saucepan over low heat, stir together caramel sauce, calvados, sea salt, and cinnamon until the mixture is warm and smooth.
2. Once fully combined, transfer the caramel mixture to a fondue pot set over a low flame to keep warm.
3. Arrange the dippers around the fondue pot, offering a delightful combination of sweet and salty to complement the rich, buttery fondue.

Nutrition information:

Nutritional value: Approximately 330 calories, 1g protein, 56g carbohydrates, 8g fats, 0g fiber, 15mg cholesterol, 350mg sodium, 85mg potassium per serving.

---

Dive into a pot where caramel and apples play the leading roles, and every dip feels like a festive fall fair. Enjoy this delectable pairing that's as comforting as a warm blanket on a crisp evening.

### 4.2.5. Recipe 17: "Velvet Raspberry Truffle Dip"

Yield: 4 servings | Preparation time: 15 minutes | Cooking time: 7 minutes.

Ingredients:

- 6 ounces dark chocolate (60-70% cacao), chopped
- 1/3 cup heavy cream
- 1/4 cup raspberry liqueur (like Chambord)
- 1 tablespoon unsalted butter
- Fresh raspberries, marshmallows, brownie bites, and shortbread cookies for dipping

Directions:

1. Gently warm the heavy cream and butter in a saucepan over low heat until the butter is melted and the cream starts to steam, being careful not to let it boil.
2. Remove the saucepan from the heat and stir in the dark chocolate until fully melted and integrated into a smooth mixture.
3. Stir in the raspberry liqueur, infusing the chocolate with a fruity zest.
4. Pour into a fondue pot, with the flame set just enough to keep it warm.
5. Serve with fresh raspberries, marshmallows, brownie bites, and shortbread cookies for an array of satisfying textures to dip and delight in.

Nutrition information:

Nutritional value: Approximately 485 calories, 4g protein, 45g carbohydrates, 32g fats, 5g fiber, 20mg cholesterol, 60mg sodium, 300mg potassium per serving.

---

This fondue is a tribute to those who love the rich taste of dark chocolate with the tangy zip of raspberries—a true tapestry of flavors weaving together in every dip.

### 4.2.6. Recipe 18: "Toasted Coconut Dream"

Yield: 4 servings | Preparation time: 10 minutes | Cooking time: 6 minutes.

Ingredients:

- 7 ounces milk chocolate, chopped
- 1/3 cup canned coconut milk, well stirred
- 2 tablespoons coconut rum
- 1/2 cup toasted shredded coconut
- Assorted dippers: pineapple chunks, mango slices, pound cake cubes, and banana slices

Directions:

1. Begin by mixing the milk chocolate and coconut milk in a saucepan over low heat, frequently stirring until the chocolate is fully melted and the mixture is smooth.
2. Add coconut rum to the saucepan and continue to stir, infusing the fondue with tropical notes.
3. Once fully integrated and warmed to satisfaction, pour the mixture into a fondue pot over a low flame to keep it temptingly dip-ready.
4. Sprinkle half of the toasted shredded coconut into the fondue and mix. Use the remaining toasted coconut to garnish the serving platter for an additional textural delight.
5. Surround your fondue pot with a colorful array of dippers like fresh tropical fruits and spongy cake, ready for a plunge into this island-inspired treat.

Nutrition information:

Nutritional value: Approximately 495 calories, 5g protein, 53g carbohydrates, 28g fats, 3g fiber, 18mg cholesterol, 75mg sodium, 330mg potassium per serving.

---

This fondue recipe is a tropical escapade in a pot, whisking you away with every dip to sandy beaches and serene sunsets. Enjoy the natural sweetness and irresistible crunch that will make any evening feel like a celebration.

## 4.2.7. Recipe 19: "Rum Rhapsody Indulgence"

Yield: 4 servings | Preparation time: 10 minutes | Cooking time: 5 minutes.

Ingredients:

- 8 ounces semi-sweet chocolate, finely chopped
- 1/2 cup heavy cream
- 3 tablespoons dark rum
- 1/2 teaspoon pure vanilla extract
- A pinch of ground nutmeg
- Assorted dippers: banana slices, pineapple chunks, pound cake cubes, and brownie bites

Directions:

1. In a saucepan over low heat, warm the heavy cream until it is hot but not boiling.
2. Gradually mix in the chopped chocolate, stirring until the chocolate is completely melted and the mixture becomes smooth.

3. Remove the saucepan from the heat and stir in the dark rum, vanilla extract, and ground nutmeg until well combined.
4. Transfer the rum-infused chocolate fondue into a fondue pot set over a low flame to keep it warm and liquid.
5. Serve with a spread of banana slices, pineapple chunks, pound cake cubes, and brownie bites perfect for a tropical, boozy dipping adventure.

Nutrition information:

Nutritional value: Approximately 470 calories, 4g protein, 45g carbohydrates, 28g fats, 3g fiber, 35mg cholesterol, 25mg sodium, 340mg potassium per serving.

---

Savor the thrill of chocolate with the rich note of dark rum, where every dip is like a symphony with a crescendo of exotic Caribbean notes—certain to captivate and bring merriment to your fondue soirée.

## 4.2.8. Recipe 20: "Wild Berry Flambe Fondue"

Yield: 4 servings | Preparation time: 10 minutes | Cooking time: 8 minutes.

Ingredients:

- 8 ounces dark chocolate (65-70% cacao), chopped
- 1/2 cup heavy cream
- 1/4 cup wild berry liqueur (like blackberry or raspberry)
- 2 tablespoons granulated sugar
- 1/2 teaspoon pure vanilla extract
- Fresh wild berries (blackberries, raspberries, strawberries), marshmallows, and sponge cake for dipping

Directions:

1. Begin by gently heating heavy cream and sugar in a saucepan over medium-low heat, stirring until the sugar dissolves and the mixture gets hot.
2. Add the chopped dark chocolate to the saucepan, stirring continuously until melted and thoroughly combined with the cream.
3. Remove the saucepan from the heat and carefully stir in the wild berry liqueur and vanilla extract.
4. Light the surface of the fondue briefly with a long match to flambe, being very careful (this should be done by an adult, kids—safety first!).
5. Once the flames subside, pour the fondue into a pot set over a low flame to keep it warm.

6. Place an assortment of fresh wild berries, marshmallows, and sponge cake pieces around the fondue pot, ready for guests to enjoy the rich and fruity dipping experience.

Nutrition information:

Nutritional value: Approximately 480 calories, 4g protein, 46g carbohydrates, 28g fats, 5g fiber, 20mg cholesterol, 25mg sodium, 350mg potassium per serving.

---

This "Wild Berry Flambe Fondue" combines the bold intensity of dark chocolate with the vibrant tang of wild berries, with an added touch of spectacle from the flambe technique. It's not just a dessert; it's an experience—rich, tangy, and with a whisper of excitement.

# 4.3. Chilled Delights: Ice Cream Fondue Fantasia

Heat reigns supreme in the realm of fondue, yet here we embrace a delightful paradox: the chilled wonders of ice cream fondue. The "Chilled Delights" sub-chapter is a whimsical waltz through frosty meadows, where creamy dollops of ice cream meet warm, cascading curtains of saccharine nectar. It's an expedition to the north pole of dessert delights, where the juxtaposition of hot and cold creates an exquisite ballet for the senses.

## 4.3.1. Recipe 21: "Chilled Cream Cascade"

Yield: 4 servings | Preparation time: 15 minutes | Cooking time: 0 minutes.

Ingredients:

- 6 ounces white chocolate, chopped
- 1/4 cup heavy cream, warmed
- 2 tablespoons flavored liqueur (such as raspberry, orange, or coffee)
- 1 pint of your favorite ice cream flavor, scoopable
- Assorted dippers: waffle cone pieces, mini cookies, fresh berries, and bite-sized brownie chunks

Directions:

1. Melt the chopped white chocolate with the warmed heavy cream in a heatproof bowl set over a pot of gently simmering water, stirring until smooth.
2. Once the white chocolate mixture is velvety, remove from heat and stir in your flavored liqueur of choice.

3. Instead of transferring to a traditional fondue pot, allow the mixture to cool slightly before drizzling it over a cold stone or chilled serving plate swirled with scoops of ice cream.
4. Surround the ice cream with your assortment of dippers for a playful, interactive dessert experience where guests can drizzle, dip, and combine creamy, frozen flavors with the luxe white chocolate sauce.

Nutrition information:

Nutritional value (chocolate sauce only): Approximately 320 calories, 3g protein, 25g carbohydrates, 22g fats, 0g fiber, 20mg cholesterol, 35mg sodium, 120mg potassium per serving.

---

Embrace a whimsical twist to fondue by introducing the cold creaminess of ice cream to the warm sweetness of melted chocolate. Dive into this reimagined fondue fantasy where classic dippers meet the chill of ice cream for an unforgettable dessert delight.

## 4.3.2. Recipe 22: "Frozen Fudge Frenzy"

Yield: 4 servings | Preparation time: 10 minutes | Cooking time: 5 minutes.

Ingredients:

- 8 ounces milk chocolate, chopped
- 1/3 cup heavy cream
- 1 tablespoon unsalted butter
- 1/2 teaspoon vanilla extract
- A small pinch of coarse sea salt
- 1-pint vanilla bean ice cream
- Assorted dippers: sliced bananas, strawberries, chunks of fudge cake, and marshmallows

Directions:

1. Heat the cream and butter in a saucepan over medium-low heat until the butter melts and the cream starts to bubble gently at the edges.
2. Remove from the heat and stir in the chopped milk chocolate until fully melted and smooth, blending in the vanilla and sea salt.
3. Let the chocolate mixture cool slightly just to a comfortable warmth suitable for ice cream.
4. Serve up bowls of vanilla bean ice cream, and drizzle with the warm milk chocolate sauce.
5. Offer guests a variety of dippers alongside their bowl for an ultimate build-your-own sundae experience with a fondue twist.

Nutrition information:

Nutritional value (chocolate sauce only): Approximately 370 calories, 3g protein, 28g carbohydrates, 26g fats, 1.5g fiber, 30mg cholesterol, 60mg sodium, 230mg potassium per serving.

---

Introducing a sumptuous classic of fondue meet ice cream—a dynamic duo sure to steal the show. Get ready to layer, dip, and drizzle your way through a sundae-inspired fondue that's both familiar and thrillingly novel.

# 4.4. A World of Flavor

Travel the globe through the fondue pot with recipes encapsulating national pride and tradition. Taste the tropics with coconut and rum, journey to Italy with amaretto, or embrace the French 'joie de vivre' with cognac-infused delights.

## 4.4.1. Recipe 23: "Samurai's Sweet Retreat"

Yield: 4 servings | Preparation time: 10 minutes | Cooking time: 5 minutes.

Ingredients:

- 8 ounces dark chocolate (60-70% cacao), chopped
- 1/2 cup heavy cream
- 1 tablespoon matcha green tea powder
- 2 tablespoons honey
- 1 tablespoon sake or plum wine
- A pinch of sea salt
- Assorted dippers: rice cracker pieces, pear slices, green tea mochi, and sponge cake

Directions:

1. Heat the heavy cream over low heat in a saucepan until it begins to simmer. Whisk in the matcha powder until fully dissolved, creating a vibrant green base.
2. Stir in the dark chocolate and honey, continually mixing until the chocolate is melted and the mixture is smooth and glossy.
3. Add the sake or plum wine and a pinch of sea salt, stirring to combine all the flavors into a bold and balanced fondue.

4. Transfer the mixture into a fondue pot set over low heat to keep it warm and ready for dipping.
5. Offer an assortment of dippers that play off the fondue's samurai-inspired flavors, like crispy rice crackers, fresh pear slices, chewy green tea mochi, and airy sponge cake.

Nutrition information:

Nutritional value: Approximately 470 calories, 5g protein, 52g carbohydrates, 28g fats, 6g fiber, 20mg cholesterol, 60mg sodium, 400mg potassium per serving.

---

"Samurai's Sweet Retreat" is a fondue that commands attention with its assertive flavors and ceremonial elegance. This recipe is an homage to the discipline and simplicity of the samurai aesthetic, combining the richness of dark chocolate with the distinct umami of matcha and a hint of sake for depth. Each dip is a taste of serene tradition with a touch of indulgence.

## 4.4.2. Recipe 24: "Hawaiian Luau Luxe"

Yield: 6 servings | Preparation time: 15 minutes | Cooking time: 5 minutes.

Ingredients:

- 8 ounces high-quality milk chocolate, chopped
- 1/2 cup coconut cream
- 2 tablespoons dark rum
- 1/4 cup crushed pineapple, drained
- 1 tablespoon light brown sugar
- A pinch of sea salt
- Assorted dippers: diced mango, papaya chunks, banana slices, macadamia nut cookies, and coconut macaroon pieces

Directions:

1. Combine coconut cream, brown sugar, and sea salt in a saucepan over medium-low heat, stirring until the sugar is dissolved.
2. Lower the heat and add the chopped milk chocolate, stirring until completely melted and smooth.
3. Stir in the dark rum and crushed pineapple, warming through to integrate the flavors.
4. Transfer the mixture into a fondue pot, maintaining a low flame to keep your Hawaiian-inspired dip warm throughout the party.

5. Prepare a tropical array of dippers like ripe mango, papaya, banana slices, crunchy macadamia nut cookies, and chewy coconut macaroons for a truly Polynesian experience.

Nutrition information:

Nutritional value: Approximately 480 calories, 4g protein, 55g carbohydrates, 26g fats, 3g fiber, 18mg cholesterol, 65mg sodium, 250mg potassium per serving.

---

The "Hawaiian Luau Luxe" is the epitome of tropical indulgence. It's rich, it's festive, and it embraces the spirit of aloha with its luscious, island-inspired flavors. This recipe makes a grand finale for any gathering that aims to impress and celebrate in a sweet, sumptuous style. Ready the leis and the ukulele—it's time to dip into paradise!

## 4.4.3. Recipe 25: "Amaretto Di Saronno Serenade"

Yield: 2 servings | Preparation time: 10 minutes | Cooking time: 5 minutes.

Ingredients:

- 6 ounces quality milk chocolate, chopped
- 1/3 cup heavy cream
- 2 tablespoons Amaretto Di Saronno liqueur
- 1/4 teaspoon pure almond extract
- A pinch of sea salt
- Vanilla or amaretto gelato, for serving
- Almond biscotti, fresh peaches, and amaretti cookies for dipping

Directions:

1. In a saucepan over low heat, combine the heavy cream and sea salt, warming gently until it starts to simmer.
2. Remove from heat and stir in the milk chocolate pieces until completely melted and incorporated into a glossy, smooth fondue.
3. Add the Amaretto Di Saronno and almond extract into the warm chocolate, stirring to unify the flavors into a fragrant delight.
4. Scoop your chosen ice cream into chilled serving bowls.
5. Invite guests to dip their almond biscotti and fresh peaches into the chocolate amaretto fondue, then onto their gelato, creating a delightful blend of textures and flavors reminiscent of a stroll through an Italian piazza.

Nutrition information:

Nutritional value: Estimated per serving—560 calories, 6g protein, 56g carbohydrates, 34g fats, 2g fiber, 70mg cholesterol, 180mg sodium, 270mg potassium.

### 4.4.4. Recipe 26: "Cognac au Chocolat Crémeux"

Yield: 2 servings | Preparation time: 10 minutes | Cooking time: 5 minutes.

Ingredients:

- 6 ounces dark chocolate (70% cacao), finely chopped
- 1/3 cup heavy cream
- 2 tablespoons Cognac
- 1 teaspoon orange zest
- A pinch of cinnamon
- Chocolate sorbet or coffee ice cream, for serving
- Madeleine cookies, orange segments, and raspberry financiers for dipping

Directions:

1. Warm the heavy cream in a saucepan over low heat until it begins to steam.
2. Remove from the heat and add the dark chocolate, whisking continuously until it's thoroughly melted into a luxurious fondue.
3. Stir in the Cognac, orange zest, and cinnamon, mixing well to ensure the aroma is laced throughout the chocolate.
4. Place scoops of chocolate sorbet or coffee ice cream into chilled dessert dishes.
5. Serve immediately alongside madeleine cookies, fresh orange segments, and raspberry financiers, encouraging a sophisticated dance of French-inspired flavors with every dip—both into the fondue and onto the ice cream.

Nutrition information:

Nutritional value: Estimated per serving—570 calories, 5g protein, 50g carbohydrates, 35g fats, 7g fiber, 20mg cholesterol, 25mg sodium, 450mg potassium.

---

These recipes transcend mere dessert status, evolving into lush, international narratives best savored slowly, with every dip, drizzle, and spoonful. Share these fondue creations, and let them inspire not just tastes of Italy and France but memories of coziness, indulgence, and pure romance.

So, my dear fellow fondue enthusiast, it's been an absolute delight to guide you through the delectable dips of our sweet-focused chapter. We've danced with spices, flirted with fruits, and twirled into the rich depths of chocolate. I hope these recipes not only tantalize your taste buds but also inspire joyous gatherings around the pot of molten sweetness.

As we bid adieu to chocolate cascades and creamy delights, we pivot to the sizzling side of fondue. Prepare your forks for a culinary crusade into the savory world of meat fondue—where the dip is hot, the bites are hearty, and the flavors are robust.

For our carnivorous chapter, let's brandish a title that embodies the sizzle and excitement of cooking each morsel to perfection:

# Chapter 5: "Meat Morsels and Sizzling Soireés"

Welcome to the sizzling domain where meat is the main act and the fondue pot is our stage. Fasten your seatbelts and sharpen your skewers; we're about to embark on a carnivore's journey filled with flavor, fun, and the fine art of dipping and cooking to perfection. Each sub-chapter will be filled with essential information, best practices, mouthwatering recipes, and of course, the engaging and light-hearted prose that you've come to love. Ready your taste buds for a meaty escapade!

## 5.1 "The Fondue Bourguignonne Ballad"

Ah, Fondue Bourguignonne—a name that rolls off the tongue as delightfully as its beefy bites roll into hot oil. Here, we celebrate this French favorite with recipes perfected over time and tips for choosing the right cuts of beef. We'll discuss everything from sirloin to tenderloin, ensuring your meat becomes the stuff of legend as it fries to perfection.

### 5.1.1. Recipe 27: "Sirloin Sizzle Soirée"

Yield: 4 servings | Preparation time: 20 minutes | Cooking time: 2-3 minutes per piece.

Ingredients:

- 1 1/2 pounds sirloin steak, trimmed of fat and cut into 1-inch cubes
- 32 ounces of canola oil or peanut oil, for frying
- Sea salt and freshly ground pepper, to taste

Herb marinade:

- 1/4 cup olive oil
- 3 cloves garlic, minced

- 2 tablespoons fresh rosemary, finely chopped
- 2 tablespoons fresh thyme, finely chopped
- 1 tablespoon Dijon mustard
- Zest of 1 lemon

Directions:

1. In a mixing bowl, combine olive oil, minced garlic, rosemary, thyme, Dijon mustard, and lemon zest for the marinade. Add the cubed sirloin to the bowl, tossing to coat. Cover and refrigerate for at least 2 hours, or overnight for deeper flavor.
2. When ready to cook, remove the beef from the refrigerator and let it come to room temperature for about 20 minutes before cooking. Season with a pinch of sea salt and freshly ground pepper.
3. In your fondue pot, heat the canola or peanut oil to 375°F (190°C). Use a candy or deep-fry thermometer to ensure the oil reaches the correct temperature for safe cooking.
4. Using fondue forks, carefully place the beef cubes into the hot oil and cook for 2-3 minutes, depending on the desired level of doneness.
5. Enjoy with a variety of dipping sauces like horseradish, béarnaise, or a peppercorn sauce.

Nutrition information:

(For sirloin and marinade only, excluding oil absorption and dipping sauces)

Nutritional value: Approximately 310 calories, 35g protein, 0g carbohydrates, 18g fats, 0g fiber, 100mg cholesterol, 80mg sodium, 450mg potassium per serving.

---

Gather your friends, crank up the jazz, and let this "Sirloin Sizzle Soirée" bring out your inner chef. Watch as the meat sizzles to succulent perfection—a simple rhapsody of richness that only a true bourguignonne experience can provide.

## 5.1.2. Recipe 28: "Peppered Filet Fondue Fantasy"

Yield: 4 servings | Preparation time: 20 minutes | Cooking time: 2-3 minutes per piece.

Ingredients:

- 1 1/2 pounds filet mignon, cut into 1-inch cubes
- 32 ounces grapeseed oil or high smoke-point oil, for frying

- 2 tablespoons coarsely ground black pepper
- Coarse sea salt to taste

Dipping sauce (Green Peppercorn Aïoli):

- 1 cup mayonnaise
- 1 tablespoon green peppercorns in brine, drained and crushed
- 2 cloves garlic, minced
- 1 tablespoon lemon juice
- Salt and a pinch of sugar, to balance the flavors

Directions:

1. Pat the filet mignon cubes dry with paper towels, then season liberally with the coarsely ground black pepper and sea salt. Let the beef sit to absorb the flavors while you heat the oil.
2. Pour the grapeseed oil into your fondue pot and heat to 375°F (190°C). Monitor the temperature with a frying thermometer to prevent overheating.
3. As the oil warms, mix the aïoli ingredients in a bowl until well combined. Set aside.
4. Once the oil reaches the correct temperature, skewer the seasoned beef cubes on fondue forks and cook in the hot oil for 2-3 minutes per piece or until it reaches your preferred level of doneness.
5. Serve immediately with the green peppercorn aïoli and additional dipping sauces, if desired.

Nutrition information:
(For filet mignon and seasonings only, excluding oil absorption and dipping sauces)

Nutritional value: Approximately 340 calories, 32g protein, 1g carbohydrates, 22g fats, 1g fiber, 110mg cholesterol, 85mg sodium, 500mg potassium per serving.

---

Indulge in a world where the premium filet mignon meets the boldness of black pepper, accompanied by the zesty tang of green peppercorn aïoli. This "Peppered Filet Fondue Fantasy" is a love letter to meat lovers who relish a touch of fiery personality with their tender, melt-in-your-mouth bites.

## 5.1.3. Recipe 29: "Garlic Herb Surf and Turf Plunge"

Yield: 4 servings | Preparation time: 30 minutes | Cooking time: 1-3 minutes per piece.

Ingredients:

- 1 pound beef tenderloin, cut into 1-inch cubes
- 1 pound large shrimp, peeled and deveined, tail-on
- 32 ounces beef broth, preferably homemade or low sodium
- 2 tablespoons mixed fresh herbs (parsley, thyme, rosemary), finely chopped
- 4 cloves garlic, minced
- Sea salt and freshly ground black pepper to taste

Garlic Herb Marinade:

- 1/3 cup olive oil
- 1/4 cup minced fresh herbs (same as above)
- 4 cloves garlic, minced
- Juice of 1 lemon
- Salt and pepper to season

Directions:

1. Combine all marinade ingredients in a bowl. Divide the marinade, using half to marinate the beef cubes and the other half for the shrimp. Refrigerate and marinate for at least 20 minutes.
2. In your fondue pot, bring the beef broth to a gentle boil. Lower the temperature to maintain a steady simmer.
3. Remove the beef and shrimp from the marinade and season both with a bit of sea salt and freshly ground black pepper.
4. Skewer the beef and shrimp separately onto fondue forks. Plunge the beef into the simmering broth and cook for 1-3 minutes depending on your desired doneness. Cook the shrimp for about 1-2 minutes per side or until they turn pink and opaque.
5. Serve immediately with a selection of dipping sauces, such as creamy horseradish, cocktail sauce, or a herbed vinaigrette.

Nutrition information:
(For beef, shrimp, and marinade only, excluding broth and dipping sauces)

Nutritional value: Approximately 350 calories, 38g protein, 2g carbohydrates, 20g fats, 0g fiber, 175mg cholesterol, 200mg sodium, 600mg potassium per serving.

---

The "Garlic Herb Surf and Turf Plunge" entwines the lush flavors of the land with the bounty of the sea, both enrobed in an aromatic marinade that pays homage to the rustic elegance of garlic and herbs. A communal pot of warm, savory broth beckons, promising adventure with every sumptuous bite into the treasures of both surf and turf.

# 5.2 "Broth Fondue Odyssey"

Lighter than oil but just as thrilling, cooking your meat in a simmering cauldron of broth is an epicurean voyage not to be missed. Whether you're creating a delicate vegetable base or a robust beef infusion, this journey through broth fondue will take you through the high seas of flavor and back with every dip.

## 5.2.1. Recipe 30: "Garden Herb Broth Bonanza"

Yield: 4 servings | Preparation time: 20 minutes (plus time for broth) | Cooking time: 1-3 minutes per piece.

Ingredients:

- 1 pound boneless skinless chicken breast, cut into 1-inch cubes
- 1 pound beef sirloin, cut into 1-inch cubes
- 48 ounces of quality chicken or beef broth
- Fresh herbs (parsley, thyme, dill), for broth and garnish
- 2 bay leaves
- 4 cloves garlic, minced
- 1 small onion, quartered
- 1 carrot, sliced
- 1 celery stalk, sliced
- Sea salt and freshly ground black pepper, to taste

Directions:

1. Begin by making your broth; combine the chicken or beef broth, fresh herbs, bay leaves, minced garlic, onion quarters, carrot, and celery in a large pot. Bring to a boil and then let it simmer for 30 minutes to enrich the flavors. Strain out the vegetables and herbs to leave a clear broth.
2. Pour the filtered broth into your fondue pot and keep it at a simmer. Season with sea salt and freshly ground black pepper.
3. Pat dry the chicken and beef cubes with paper towels. Skewer the meats separately onto fondue forks and cook in the simmering broth until the chicken is no longer pink (about 2-3 minutes) and the beef is cooked to the desired doneness (1-3 minutes).
4. Serve with a variety of dipping sauces—try a tangy yogurt dill sauce for the chicken and a robust mustard sauce for the beef. Garnish with additional fresh herbs for that garden-fresh touch.

Nutrition information:

Nutritional value (for chicken, beef, and broth only, excluding sauces): Approximately 240 calories, 36g protein, 3g carbohydrates, 8g fats, 1g fiber, 85mg cholesterol, 600mg sodium, 650mg potassium per serving.

The "Garden Herb Broth Bonanza" beckons you to a paradise of flavor where the clear, seasoned broth harmonizes with fresh garden herbs. Each bite of delicately cooked meat, infused with the subtle tastes of nature's seasonings, promises a symphony of savor to awaken the senses.

## 5.2.2. Recipe 31: "Asian Infusion Elixir"

Yield: 4 servings | Preparation time: 25 minutes (plus time for broth) | Cooking time: 1-3 minutes per piece.

Ingredients:

- 1 pound thinly sliced beef sirloin or shabu-shabu style beef
- 1 pound boneless pork loin, thinly sliced
- 48 ounces of quality vegetable or beef broth
- 3 tablespoons soy sauce
- 2 tablespoons mirin (Japanese sweet rice wine)
- 2-inch piece of ginger, sliced
- 3 green onions, chopped
- 2 garlic cloves, minced
- 1 teaspoon sesame oil
- 1/2 teaspoon red pepper flakes (optional for heat)
- Fresh cilantro and sliced mushrooms for garnish

Directions:

1. To prepare the broth, combine the vegetable or beef broth with soy sauce, mirin, ginger slices, chopped green onions, minced garlic, sesame oil, and red pepper flakes in a large pot. Bring to a low boil and then reduce to a simmer for 20 minutes.
2. Strain the broth to remove solid pieces and pour it into your fondue pot. Keep the broth simmering gently.
3. Arrange the thinly sliced beef and pork on separate plates, keeping them ready for cooking.
4. Use fondue forks to carefully dip and swirl the meat slices in the hot broth. Cook the beef and pork slices until they are cooked through, typically 1-3 minutes, depending on the thickness of the slices and desired doneness.
5. Serve the cooked slices with a selection of dipping sauces, such as hoisin sauce, chili sauce, or a sesame dipping sauce. Garnish the pot with fresh cilantro and sliced mushrooms before serving for a fully aromatic experience.

Nutrition information:

Nutritional value (for beef, pork, and the seasoned broth only, excluding additional sauces): Approximately 250 calories, 38g protein, 5g carbohydrates, 7g fats, 1g fiber, 90mg cholesterol, 900mg sodium, 700mg potassium per serving.

---

"Asian Infusion Elixir" is a fondue that echoes the timeless tradition of Eastern cuisine, blending the complex flavors of soy, mirin, and spices. Each tender slice of meat absorbs the soul-warming essence of the broth, providing a delectable journey through the essence of Asia with each bite.

### 5.2.3. Recipe 32: "Mediterranean Meld Pot"

Yield: 4 servings | Preparation time: 30 minutes (plus time for broth) | Cooking time: 1-3 minutes per piece.

Ingredients:

- 1 pound lamb tenderloin, cut into 1-inch cubes
- 48 ounces of chicken or vegetable broth
- 1 large onion, quartered
- 4 cloves of garlic, smashed
- 1 sprig rosemary
- 1 sprig thyme
- 1 lemon, zest peeled in strips
- 1 teaspoon whole peppercorns
- 1 tablespoon olive oil
- Sea salt to taste
- Fresh mint, chopped for garnish

Directions:

1. Prepare the broth in a large pot by combining chicken or vegetable broth, onion quarters, smashed garlic, rosemary, thyme, strips of lemon zest, whole peppercorns, and a drizzle of olive oil. Bring to a simmer and let it infuse for 30 minutes, then strain to remove the solids.
2. Transfer the fragrant broth to your fondue pot, keeping the heat enough to maintain a gentle simmer.
3. Season the cubed lamb tenderloin with sea salt. Keep the pieces chilled until ready to fondue.
4. Skewer the lamb cubes on fondue forks and cook them in the simmering broth until they reach the desired level of doneness, typically 1-3 minutes depending on personal preference.

5. Serve with a variety of Mediterranean-inspired dipping sauces such as tzatziki, a mint yogurt sauce, or a red pepper hummus. Sprinkle with fresh mint for an additional burst of freshness.

Nutrition information:

Nutritional value: Approximately 310 calories, 40g protein, 0g carbohydrates, 16g fats, 0g fiber, 120mg cholesterol, 600mg sodium, 460mg potassium per serving.

---

Bask in the warmth of the Mediterranean sun with our "Mediterranean Meld Pot," where succulent lamb cozies up to an aromatic broth that whispers tales of fragrant herbs and zestful lemon. Each dip becomes a journey through sunny landscapes and moonlit seas—a vibrant escape in every tender, herb-kissed bite.

## 5.3. "Chinoiserie Chic – The Asian Hot Pot Expedition"

Don your explorers' hat as we take a detour to the Far East. We'll map out the traditions of the Asian hot pot—from choosing the right equipment to selecting a medley of meats and complementary vegetables and noodles. Discover how this fondue variety can turn your meal into an interactive culinary exploration.

### 5.3.1. Recipe 33: "1001 Eastern Nights Hot Pot"

Yield: 6 servings | Preparation time: 30 minutes (plus time for broth) | Cooking time: 1-3 minutes per piece.

Ingredients:

- 1 pound thinly sliced beef shoulder
- 1 pound chicken breast, thinly sliced
- 48 ounces dashi broth or mild chicken broth
- 2 tablespoons soy sauce
- 1 tablespoon sake
- 2 teaspoons sugar
- 2 inches ginger root, thinly sliced
- 2 star anise pods
- 1 cinnamon stick
- 1 bunch scallions, sliced into 2-inch pieces
- 1 bunch bok choy, separated into leaves
- Sea salt and white pepper to taste

Dipping Sauces:

- Goma Dare (Sesame Sauce)
- Ponzu Sauce

- Spicy Sichuan Sauce

Accompaniments:

- Udon noodles, cooked and cooled
- Enoki mushrooms
- Thinly sliced carrots and daikon radishes
- Fresh cilantro and sesame seeds for garnish

Directions:

1. Begin by preparing the flavorful broth in a large pot. Combine dashi broth, soy sauce, sake, sugar, ginger slices, star anise pods, cinnamon sticks, and scallions. Bring to a simmer and let it infuse for 20-30 minutes. Strain the broth to remove the solid ingredients and maintain a gentle simmer in your hot pot vessel.
2. Arrange the thinly sliced beef and chicken on serving platters alongside the prepared vegetables and noodles.
3. Invite guests to use the fondue skewers or hot pot strainers to cook the meat and vegetable slices in the simmering broth, typically for 1-2 minutes for meats and just a minute for the vegetables.
4. Prepare small bowls with the selected dipping sauces for each guest. The goma dare sesame sauce adds nutty depth, the ponzu offers a citrus kick, and the spicy Sichuan sauce brings the heat for those who dare.
5. Serve the cooked meats and vegetables over the bed of udon noodles, letting the broth imbibe everything with its rich flavor. Garnish with fresh cilantro and a sprinkle of sesame seeds for a fragrant finish.

Nutrition information:

Nutritional value (for meats, vegetables, and broth only, excluding dipping sauces and accompaniments): Approximately 240 calories, 35g protein, 6g carbohydrates, 9g fats, 1g fiber, 80mg cholesterol, 800mg sodium, 650mg potassium per serving.

---

Embrace the exotic allure of the Far East with the "1001 Eastern Nights Hot Pot," a traditional feast where the communal joy of cooking is as savored as the flavors themselves. Every ingredient, from the delicately sliced meats to the fresh crisp vegetables, becomes an ode to the enchanting nights of timeless tales and Eastern mystique.

## 5.3.2. Recipe 34: "Aladdin's Aromatic Adventure"

Yield: 4 servings | Preparation time: 25 minutes (plus time for broth) | Cooking time: 1-3 minutes per piece.

Ingredients:

- 1 pound lamb shoulder, thinly sliced
- 1 pound large shrimp, peeled and deveined
- 48 ounces chicken or vegetable broth
- 3 tablespoons oyster sauce
- 1 tablespoon hoisin sauce
- 2 teaspoons sesame oil
- 3 cloves garlic, minced
- 1 piece star anise
- 1 cinnamon stick
- 2 cardamom pods
- Fresh mint and cilantro for garnish

Dipping Sauces:

- Chili Garlic Sauce
- Mint Yogurt Dip
- Tamarind Sauce

Accompaniments:

- Vermicelli rice noodles, cooked and cooled
- Thinly sliced bell peppers, zucchini, and eggplant
- Diced pineapple and mango for a sweet contrast

Directions:

1. Create a broth imbued with the flavors of Agrabah by combining the broth with oyster sauce, hoisin sauce, sesame oil, garlic, star anise, cinnamon, and cardamom in a large pot. Bring to a simmer for 20 minutes, then strain the broth into your hot pot, keeping it at a low simmer.
2. Display the lamb and shrimp attractively on platters, alongside the prepared vegetables and fruits.
3. Guests can cook their meats and veggies in the simmering broth using hot pot strainers or fondue forks, cooking the lamb to desired doneness and the shrimp until pink and opaque, typically 1-3 minutes.
4. Provide a selection of dipping sauces that complement the richness of the meats and the freshness of the vegetables. Chili for heat, mint yogurt for a cooling effect, and tamarind for a tangy twist.

5. Arrange the vermicelli noodles in individual bowls, allowing guests to add their cooked ingredients on top, creating their own personalized Aladdin's feast. Garnish with a sprinkle of fresh mint and cilantro leaves for added freshness.

Nutrition information:

Nutritional value (for meats, vegetables, and fruit only, with broth, excluding sauces and noodles): Approximately 260 calories, 30g protein, 10g carbohydrates, 12g fats, 2g fiber, 150mg cholesterol, 700mg sodium, 480mg potassium per serving.

---

"Aladdin's Aromatic Adventure" transports you to the bustling markets and enchanted evenings of old Arabian nights, with each ingredient telling a tale of flavor and festivity. This hot pot recipe is a magical carpet ride across a culinary landscape rich with the fragrant and savory spices of the East—a feast where every bite is a discovery.

## 5.3.3. Recipe 35: "Pharaoh's Feast Broth Pot"

Yield: 4 servings | Preparation time: 25 minutes (plus time for broth) | Cooking time: 1-3 minutes per piece.

Ingredients:

- 1 pound filet mignon, thinly sliced
- 1 pound chicken tenders, thinly sliced
- 48 ounces beef broth
- 2 teaspoons ground cumin
- 2 teaspoons coriander seeds
- 1 teaspoon paprika
- 1/4 teaspoon ground cinnamon
- Zest of 1 orange
- 4 dates, pitted and chopped
- Fresh parsley and dill, chopped for garnish

Dipping Sauces:

- Spiced Honey Garlic Sauce
- Creamy Dill Tahini
- Citrus Harissa Blend

Accompaniments:

- Pita bread, cut into wedges

- Assorted fresh vegetables: carrots, bell peppers, and asparagus
- Dried apricots and figs for a sweet addition

Directions:

1. Bring the beef broth to a simmer in a large pot, add cumin, coriander seeds, paprika, cinnamon, and orange zest. Let the flavors meld for 20 minutes, adding the chopped dates during the last 5 minutes for a subtle sweetness.
2. Strain the spiced broth to remove solid pieces and transfer it to your hot pot set on a low simmer.
3. Arrange the thinly sliced filet mignon and chicken on separate plates for your guests.
4. Guests can use fondue forks to cook their slices of meat in the hot, spiced broth, usually just a minute or two until desired doneness is achieved.
5. Serve with dipping sauces that complement the Pharaoh-inspired spices: a sweet and tangy honey garlic sauce, a smooth dill tahini, and a vibrant citrus harissa blend for a spicy kick.
6. Place pita wedges, fresh vegetables, and dried fruits around the hot pot for additional dipping and flavor combinations.

Nutrition information:

Nutritional value (for meats and broth with spices only, excluding dipping sauces and accompaniments): Approximately 285 calories, 38g protein, 5g carbohydrates, 12g fats, 1g fiber, 105mg cholesterol, 300mg sodium, 700mg potassium per serving.

---

With "Pharaoh's Feast Broth Pot," we transport you back to ancient Egypt, where royalty dined on the finest of meats infused with spices traded along the Nile. This hot pot stands as an edible pyramid, with layers of flavors built to enchant modern-day pharaohs and queens alike. Enjoy this regal and communal dining adventure, fit for a banquet in a grand temple.

## 5.4. "Poultry Playhouse"

Who says beef and seafood get to have all the fun? It's time for chicken and turkey to take the spotlight. Lean yet savory, poultry is perfect for those who prefer their fondue a bit on the lighter side. Learn how to marinate with herbs and citrus to make your feathered feast fly off the forks.

### 5.4.1. Recipe 36: "Tuscan Chicken Brodo Dip"

Yield: 4 servings | Preparation time: 20 minutes | Cooking time: 2-3 minutes per piece.

Ingredients:

- 1 pound boneless skinless chicken breast, cut into 1-inch cubes
- 48 ounces chicken broth
- 2 cloves of garlic, smashed
- 1 teaspoon dried Italian herbs (basil, oregano, thyme)
- 1 small sprig of rosemary
- 1/2 cup diced tomatoes (canned or fresh)
- Salt and freshly ground black pepper to taste
- Fresh basil and grated Parmesan cheese for garnish

Directions:

1. In a large pot, combine the chicken broth, smashed garlic cloves, dried Italian herbs, rosemary sprig, diced tomatoes, salt, and pepper. Bring the mixture to a gentle simmer, allowing the flavors to meld for about 15 minutes.
2. Strain the broth to remove the herbs and garlic, then transfer the clear, seasoned broth to your fondue pot, keeping it at a simmer.
3. Pat the chicken cubes dry, season them with salt and pepper, and arrange them on a platter.
4. Guests can lightly cook their chicken pieces in the hot broth using fondue forks until the chicken is cooked through, about 2-3 minutes.
5. Once cooked, they can sprinkle fresh basil and grated Parmesan cheese over their chicken for a burst of Tuscan flavor.

Nutrition information:

Nutritional value (for chicken and broth only, excluding garnishes): Approximately 230 calories, 38g protein, 2g carbohydrates, 6g fats, 0g fiber, 80mg cholesterol, 500mg sodium, 420mg potassium per serving.

---

Let "Tuscan Chicken Brodo Dip" transport you to the rolling hills and rustic kitchens of Tuscany with every tender piece of chicken. Soak up the simple and wholesome flavors of the Italian countryside and enjoy a communal meal that's both comforting and heartwarming.

## 5.4.2. Recipe 37: "Lemongrass Coq au Ginger Plunge"

Yield: 4 servings | Preparation time: 15 minutes | Cooking time: 2-3 minutes per piece.

Ingredients:

- 1 pound chicken thighs, skinless and boneless, cut into 1-inch chunks
- 48 ounces of water

- 2 stalks of lemongrass, bruised and chopped
- 4 slices of ginger
- 2 cloves of garlic, crushed
- 1 medium onion, quartered
- 1 small bunch cilantro stems (reserve leaves for garnish)
- 1 lime, juiced
- Salt to taste

Directions:

1. Prepare the broth by bringing water to a boil and adding lemongrass, ginger, garlic, onion, and cilantro stems for a fragrantly refreshing base. Lower to a simmer for 20 minutes to allow the flavors to infuse.
2. Strain the aromatics from the broth, then stir in the lime juice and adjust with salt for a balanced seasoning. Pour the broth into your fondue pot and keep it warm on a low flame.
3. Disperse the chicken thigh chunks on a serving plate. When ready, guests can submerge each piece into the hot lemongrass-ginger broth with fondue forks, letting the chicken cook until fully done, typically 2-3 minutes per piece.
4. Serve the cooked poultry with dipping sauces like sweet chili sauce or soy-based dipping sauce. Garnish the pot or individual portions with fresh cilantro leaves for a herby finish.

Nutrition information:

Nutritional value (for chicken and broth only, excluding dipping sauces): Approximately 210 calories, 30g protein, 3g carbohydrates, 9g fats, 0g fiber, 100mg cholesterol, 420mg sodium, 370mg potassium per serving.

---

The "Lemongrass Coq au Ginger Plunge" melds the zesty twang of lemongrass with the warm spice of ginger, creating a light yet flavorsome broth perfect for cooking delicate pieces of chicken. Let each dip and swirl of the fondue fork immerse you in a taste experience that's rooted in the aromatic cuisine of Southeast Asia.

## 5.4.3. Recipe 38: "Herb-Infused Turkey Temptation"

Yield: 4 servings | Preparation time: 20 minutes | Cooking time: 2-3 minutes per piece.

Ingredients:

- 1 pound turkey breast, cut into 1-inch cubes
- 48 ounces of low-sodium chicken broth

- 1 tablespoon olive oil
- 1 teaspoon dried sage
- 1 teaspoon dried thyme
- 2 bay leaves
- 1 apple, chopped
- Salt and freshly ground black pepper, to taste
- Fresh parsley, finely chopped for garnish

Directions:

1. In a large pot over medium heat, warm the olive oil and then add dried sage, thyme, and bay leaves. Toast the herbs slightly until fragrant.
2. Pour in the chicken broth and bring to a gentle simmer. Add the chopped apple to the broth and allow the flavors to meld together for 15-20 minutes.
3. Strain the broth to remove the apple pieces and herbs, then transfer it to your fondue pot, maintaining a low simmering temperature.
4. Season the turkey breast cubes with salt and pepper, then arrange them on a platter ready for cooking.
5. Guests can cook the turkey in the simmering broth using fondue forks until the meat is no longer pink and is cooked through about 2-3 minutes.
6. Sprinkle with freshly chopped parsley before serving alongside your favorite dipping sauces, such as a tangy cranberry chutney or a creamy garlic aioli.

Nutrition information:

Nutritional value (for turkey and broth only, excluding dipping sauces): Approximately 185 calories, 33g protein, 1g carbohydrates, 4g fats, 0g fiber, 65mg cholesterol, 375mg sodium, 400mg potassium per serving.

---

The "Herb-Infused Turkey Temptation" brings a humble elegance to your fondue feast with its gentle palette of flavors. The subtle, earthy tones of sage and thyme, combined with the sweetness of apple-infused broth, provide a perfect bath for tender turkey morsels—creating a warm and comforting dish that's as suitable for festive occasions as it is for a casual dining affair.

## 5.5. "Game Day - Exotic Meats and Novel Treats"

Welcome to the wild side where the exotic becomes the everyday. This chapter is dedicated to the adventurous eater looking to dabble in game meats like venison, bison, and even ostrich. Dive into the art of cooking these meats and making your fondue an out-of-the-ordinary event. With their unique flavors and textures, these novel treats promise an adventurous dining experience, evoking the spirit of a safari with every sizzling bite. Let's don our chef hats and get ready to cook up something truly extraordinary for our "Game Day - Exotic Meats and Novel Treats" chapter.

### 5.5.1. Recipe 39: "Savannah Venison Sizzle"

Yield: 4 servings | Preparation time: 30 minutes | Cooking time: 2-3 minutes per piece.

Ingredients:

- 1 pound venison loin, cut into 1-inch cubes
- 32 ounces beef or game broth
- 2 sprigs fresh rosemary
- 2 cloves garlic, minced
- 1/2 teaspoon juniper berries, crushed (optional)
- Sea salt and freshly ground black pepper, to taste
- Wild berry compote or red wine reduction, for dipping

Directions:

1. Start by preparing the fondue broth. Combine the beef or game broth with rosemary sprigs, minced garlic, and crushed juniper berries in a pot. Bring it to a simmer for 15-20 minutes to marry the flavors.
2. Strain the aromatics from the broth, pour into your fondue pot, and maintain a steady simmer.
3. Season the venison cubes with sea salt and freshly ground black pepper. Arrange them on a serving platter.
4. Use fondue forks to cook the venison cubes in the hot broth to the desired doneness, typically 2-3 minutes for medium-rare.
5. Offer the wild berry compote or a rich red wine reduction as dipping sauces to complement the robust flavors of the game meat.

Nutrition information:

Nutritional value (for venison and broth only, excluding dipping sauces): Approximately 220 calories, 38g protein, 0g carbohydrates, 3g fats, 0g fiber, 95mg cholesterol, 390mg sodium, 610mg potassium per serving.

### 5.5.2. Recipe 40: "Bison Broth Fondue Frontier"

Yield: 4 servings | Preparation time: 25 minutes | Cooking time: 2-3 minutes per piece.

Ingredients:

- 1 pound bison sirloin, cut into 1-inch cubes
- 32 ounces chicken or vegetable broth
- 2 tablespoons Worcestershire sauce
- 1 tablespoon smoked paprika

- 1 teaspoon dry mustard
- Salt and coarse ground black pepper, to taste
- Chimichurri or horseradish cream sauce, for dipping

Directions:

1. In a pot, mix together the broth, Worcestershire sauce, smoked paprika, and dry mustard. Bring the mixture to a simmer and let it cook for 10-15 minutes for the flavors to infuse.
2. Pour the seasoned broth into the fondue pot and keep it simmering lightly.
3. Season the bison cubes with salt and pepper, and arrange them on a plate.
4. Guests can now cook their bison to their preference in the broth, usually around 2-3 minutes for medium-rare, using fondue forks.
5. Serve with dips such as chimichurri for a herby freshness or horseradish cream for a sharp, contrasting flavor.

Nutrition information:

Nutritional value (for bison and broth only, excluding dipping sauces): Approximately 240 calories, 36g protein, 1g carbohydrates, 8g fats, 0g fiber, 80mg cholesterol, 500mg sodium, 640mg potassium per serving.

---

These recipes not only bring a taste of the wild to your table but also provide a foray into the elegant simplicity of cooking game meats. These noble proteins, with their deep flavors, promise a culinary adventure as rich and untamed as the lands they roam. Enjoy the feast and the many stories it will inspire around your fondue pot!

### 5.5.3. Recipe 41: "Outback Ostrich Oasis"

Yield: 4 servings | Preparation time: 25 minutes | Cooking time: 2-3 minutes per piece.

Ingredients:

- 1 pound ostrich fillet, cut into 1-inch cubes
- 32 ounces of chicken or beef broth
- 1 teaspoon black peppercorns
- 1 sprig of thyme
- 1 clove of garlic, crushed
- 1/2 teaspoon coriander seeds
- Sea salt to taste
- Exotic mushroom sauce or balsamic reduction, for dipping

Directions:

1. Prepare the broth by pouring it into a pot and adding black peppercorns, a sprig of thyme, crushed garlic clove, and coriander seeds. Simmer the broth for 20 minutes to let the spices and herbs infuse their flavors.
2. Strain the broth, remove the solids, and transfer it to your fondue pot, keeping it simmering.
3. Season the ostrich cubes with sea salt, then spread them onto a plate.
4. Using fondue forks, cook the ostrich pieces in the hot broth for 2-3 minutes or until they're cooked to your liking. Ostrich meat is best-enjoyed medium to medium-rare.
5. Serve the cooked ostrich with an exotic mushroom sauce to complement its rich flavor, or with a balsamic reduction for a sweet and tangy contrast.

Nutrition information:

Nutritional value (for ostrich and broth only, excluding dipping sauces): Approximately 150 calories, 22g protein, 0g carbohydrates, 6g fats, 0g fiber, 58mg cholesterol, 480mg sodium, 360mg potassium per serving.

---

"Outback Ostrich Oasis" guides you through a culinary expedition with a taste of the Australian wild. Lean and tender with a full-bodied flavor, ostrich fondue is an exotic and luxurious twist to the traditional fondue set. It's an invitation to expand your palate and explore the extraordinary, creating an unforgettable dining escapade that your taste buds will relish.

## 5.6. "Sauté and Savor – The Fondue Chinoise Chronicles"

Fondue Chinoise offers a symphony of delicate tastes, with thinly sliced meats and a subtle stock that sings with flavor. This dance of textures and temperatures requires finesse, and you'll be guided every step of the way to achieve that perfect tender dip.

### 5.6.1. Recipe 42: "East Asian Elegance Broth"

Yield: 4 servings | Preparation time: 20 minutes (plus time for broth to cool) | Cooking time: 2-3 minutes per piece.

Ingredients:

- 1 pound thinly sliced beef tenderloin
- 1 pound thinly sliced chicken breast
- 48 ounces of water
- 4 dried shiitake mushrooms
- 2 green onions, roughly chopped

- 3 slices of ginger
- 2 cloves of garlic, smashed
- 1 star anise
- 1 tablespoon soy sauce
- 1 teaspoon sesame oil
- Salt to taste
- Fresh greens like bok choy or spinach, for serving
- A selection of dipping sauces (e.g., ponzu, sesame, chili oil)

Directions:

1. To prepare the broth, bring water to a boil and add shiitake mushrooms, green onions, ginger, garlic, star anise, soy sauce, and sesame oil. Simmer for 30 minutes, allowing the flavors to develop fully.
2. Let the broth cool slightly, strain, then transfer it into your fondue pot and keep it at a soft simmer.
3. Arrange the beef and chicken slices on separate platters.
4. Guests may then use fondue forks or mesh strainers to cook their slices of meat in the hot broth, about 1-2 minutes for the beef and 2-3 minutes for the chicken.
5. Serve the broth pot with fresh greens for dunking and cooking in the simmering liquid, plus a selection of dipping sauces for a dynamic taste experience.

Nutrition information:

Nutritional value (for meat and broth only, excluding dipping sauces and vegetables): Approximately 230 calories, 35g protein, 1g carbohydrates, 8g fats, 0g fiber, 80mg cholesterol, 500mg sodium, 620mg potassium per serving.

---

Dining on "East Asian Elegance Broth" is a serene experience, bringing the balance and beauty of East Asian flavors to your table. Like brush strokes on rice paper, the subtlety of the spiced and aromatic broth complements the delicately cooked meats for a meal that's as artful as it is appetizing.

## 5.6.2. Recipe 43: "Shabu-Shabu Symphony"

Yield: 4 servings | Preparation time: 25 minutes | Cooking time: 1-2 minutes per piece.

Ingredients:

- 1 pound paper-thin sliced pork loin or ribeye
- 48 ounces clear kombu (kelp) stock

- 1/4 cup sake
- 1 tablespoon mirin
- Assorted fresh vegetables, thinly sliced (carrots, baby bok choy, mushrooms)
- Udon noodles, pre-cooked
- Dipping sauces such as citrusy ponzu, goma (sesame), and spicy miso

Directions:

1. Combine the kombu stock, sake, and mirin in a pot. Bring it to a light simmer, then transfer the broth to your fondue pot, maintaining a low simmer.
2. Plate the sliced pork (or beef) and arrange the sliced vegetables neatly on a serving platter.
3. Invite guests to cook their own slices in the broth using chopsticks or fondue strainers, just until they are cooked (shabu-shabu means "swish-swish" for the quick action needed).
4. Set out pre-cooked udon noodles to be warmed in the broth and eaten with the cooked meat and vegetables.
5. Serve a trio of dipping sauces on the side, allowing each dip to add complex flavors to the tender, boiled meat and vegetables.

Nutrition information:

Nutritional value (for pork, broth, and mirin only, excluding dipping sauces, vegetables, and noodles): Approximately 225 calories, 35g protein, 1g carbohydrates, 9g fats, 0g fiber, 85mg cholesterol, 650mg sodium, 600mg potassium per serving.

---

The "Shabu-Shabu Symphony" creates a harmonious interplay between delicate slices of meat, fresh vegetables, and a light but flavorful broth. It's an interactive culinary concert, where each participant weaves their own blend of flavors, creating a dining experience that's both personal and shared.

# 5.7. "Surf's Up! - Seafood and Fondue Harmony"

A seaside twist to the usual fondue fare, we'll be swimming through the steps of preparing seafood for fondue—from the delicate timing of cooking shrimp and scallops to handling sturdier fish like salmon and tuna.

### 5.7.1. Recipe 44: "Neptune's Nectar Seafood Pot"

Yield: 4 servings | Preparation time: 30 minutes | Cooking time: 1-5 minutes per piece, depending on the seafood.

Ingredients:

- 1/2 pound large shrimp, peeled and deveined, tails on
- 1/2 pound sea scallops, muscle removed
- 1/2 pound salmon filet, skinless, cut into 1-inch cubes
- 1/2 pound firm white fish like cod or halibut, cut into 1-inch cubes
- 48 ounces seafood or vegetable broth
- 2 tbsp dry white wine
- 2 cloves garlic, minced
- 1 lemon, sliced, plus more for garnish
- 1 tsp Old Bay seasoning
- Fresh dill and parsley, chopped for garnish
- Assorted dipping sauces: cocktail, tartar, remoulade

Directions:

1. In a large pot, combine the broth, white wine, minced garlic, slices of lemon, and Old Bay seasoning. Bring to a gentle simmer for 20 minutes to blend the flavors.
2. Transfer the seasoned broth to your fondue pot and maintain a low simmer.
3. Arrange the shrimp, scallops, salmon, and white fish cubes on a chilled platter.
4. Guests can cook their seafood in the broth using fondue forks or mesh strainers, just until done: shrimp and scallops for about 2 minutes until opaque, salmon for about 3 minutes until flaky, and white fish for about 3-5 minutes depending on thickness.
5. Serve your divine dip with lemon slices and fresh herbs for garnish, and a selection of classic seafood sauces on the side for added zest and flavor.

Nutrition information:

Nutritional value (for seafood and broth only, excluding dipping sauces): Approximately 190 calories, 26g protein, 1g carbohydrates, 8g fats, 0g fiber, 60mg cholesterol, 480mg sodium, 450mg potassium per serving.

## 5.7.2. Recipe 45: "Lobster Lagoon Fondue"

Yield: 4 servings | Preparation time: 20 minutes | Cooking time: 3-4 minutes per piece.

Ingredients:

- 2 whole lobsters, about 1 1/2 pounds each, parboiled and cut into large chunks
- 48 ounces court-bouillon or fish stock
- 1 fennel bulb, thinly sliced
- 1/2 cup dry vermouth

- 2 sprigs tarragon
- 1 shallot, minced
- Salt and freshly cracked black pepper to taste
- Drawn butter and lemon wedges for dipping

Directions:

1. Combine the court-bouillon or fish stock, sliced fennel, dry vermouth, tarragon sprigs, and minced shallot in a pot. Season with salt and pepper, then bring to a simmer for 15 minutes to marry the flavors.
2. Carefully strain the broth into your fondue pot, keeping it hot for cooking.
3. Present the parboiled lobster chunks on a serving tray; since they are partly cooked, they will only need a brief dip in the fondue to heat through.
4. Invite guests to submerge the lobster pieces in the simmering broth using fondue forks, cooking them for 3-4 minutes, just until heated thoroughly.
5. Accompany this luxurious fondue with small dishes of warm, drawn butter and wedges of lemon for squeezing over the lobster.

Nutrition information:

Nutritional value (for lobster and court-bouillon only, excluding drawn butter and lemon): Approximately 210 calories, 24g protein, 2g carbohydrates, 10g fats, 0g fiber, 95mg cholesterol, 460mg sodium, 300mg potassium per serving.

---

The "Lobster Lagoon Fondue" is a dive into decadence, with rich lobsters taking a second dip into a simmering pot of aromatic court-bouillon. This fondue is about indulging in the finer things in life, a true treasure trove of taste from the depths of Neptune's kingdom.


## 5.7.3. Recipe 46: "Giant Crab Gala"

Yield: 4 servings | Preparation time: 15 minutes | Cooking time: 2-5 minutes per piece.

Ingredients:

- 2 whole giant crabs (such as king or snow crab), pre-cooked, cleaned, and shells cracked
- 1/2 pound scallops
- 1/2 pound shrimp, peeled and deveined
- 48 ounces seasoned seafood broth
- 1 lemon, sliced
- 2 sprigs fresh dill

- 2 sprigs fresh tarragon
- 1 teaspoon whole black peppercorns
- Salt to taste
- Melted butter and lemon wedges for serving
- Optional: a splash of brandy or sherry to the broth

Directions:

1. Prepare the seafood broth by bringing it to a simmer with the lemon slices, dill, tarragon, and black peppercorns. Add the brandy or sherry if using. Let the flavors infuse for around 10 minutes.
2. Gently pour the broth into your fondue pot, and adjust to maintain a simmer.
3. Arrange the giant crab pieces on a large serving plate alongside scallops and shrimp.
4. Guests can use fondue forks or specially designed shellfish tongs to warm the crab in the broth, about 3-5 minutes since it's already pre-cooked. Cook the scallops for about 2 minutes until opaque, and the shrimp until they're pink and firm, about 2-3 minutes.
5. Serve the steaming seafood with dishes of melted butter for dipping and additional lemon wedges for a zesty finish.

Nutrition information:

Nutritional value (for seafood and broth only, excluding melted butter): Approximately 250 calories, 38g protein, 0g carbohydrates, 6g fats, 0g fiber, 85mg cholesterol, 600mg sodium, 450mg potassium per serving.

Dip into opulence with the "Giant Crab Gala," a celebration where the sweet, succulent flesh of a giant crab reigns supreme. The delicate accompaniment of shrimp and scallops serves to crown the crab's regal flavor, all bathed in a courtly seasoned broth. Craft an unforgettable culinary event, perfect for holidays, special occasions, or whenever you yearn for a dip into the lap of luxury.

## 5.7.4. Recipe 47: "Mariner's Mélange Mingle"

Yield: 4 servings | Preparation time: 20 minutes | Cooking time: 1-5 minutes per piece.

Ingredients:

- 1/2 pound mussels, cleaned and debearded
- 1/2 pound oysters, shucked
- 1/2 pound calamari, sliced into rings
- 48 ounces light seafood broth or white wine court-bouillon

- 1/4 cup dry white wine
- 2 bay leaves
- 1 teaspoon fennel seeds
- A pinch of saffron threads
- Salt and freshly cracked black pepper to taste
- Fresh parsley and lemon slices for garnish
- Aioli and marinara sauce for dipping

Directions:

1. In a large pot, infuse the seafood broth or court-bouillon with dry white wine, bay leaves, fennel seeds, and saffron threads. Season with salt and pepper, and simmer for 15 minutes to allow the flavors to combine.
2. Strain the aromatics from the broth and pour the liquid into the fondue pot, keeping it at a gentle simmer.
3. Arrange the mussels, oysters, and calamari rings on separate plates.
4. Guests can cook the seafood in the prepared broth: mussels until they open, about 1-3 minutes; oysters just until the edges curl, about 2 minutes; and calamari for no more than 1-2 minutes to keep it tender.
5. Serve with lemon wedges for squeezing and chopped parsley for garnish. Offer aioli and marinara sauce for dipping to complement the seafood's fresh, briny flavors.

Nutrition information:

Nutritional value (for seafood and broth only, excluding dipping sauces): Approximately 180 calories, 20g protein, 10g carbohydrates, 4g fats, 0g fiber, 50mg cholesterol, 300mg sodium, 400mg potassium per serving.

---

"Mariner's Mélange Mingle" invites you to explore the treasure chest of the ocean's offerings. Mussels, oysters, and calamari dance in a pot of subtly saffron-infused broth, teasing out flavors that are as deep and mysterious as the sea itself. Every skewer plunged into the boiling brew symbolizes a dip net into the sea, emerging with a catch that's perfectly poached and ready to send your taste buds sailing.

## 5.7.5. Recipe 48: "Ocean Trio Spectacle"

Yield: 4 servings | Preparation time: 20 minutes | Cooking time: 1-5 minutes per piece.

Ingredients:

- 1/2 pound octopus, cleaned and tenderized, cut into bite-sized pieces
- 1/2 pound cuttlefish, cleaned, with body sliced into rings and tentacles halved

- 1/2 pound langoustines, whole
- 48 ounces light fish stock or court-bouillon
- 1/4 cup white wine
- 2 cloves garlic, minced
- 1 tablespoon parsley, finely chopped
- 1 teaspoon dried oregano
- 1/2 teaspoon red chili flakes (optional for heat)
- Salt and freshly cracked black pepper to taste
- Aioli and spicy tomato sauce for dipping

Directions:

1. Create an aromatic base for your seafood by combining fish stock, white wine, minced garlic, parsley, oregano, and chili flakes in a large pot. Season with salt and pepper, and bring the mixture to a gentle simmer for about 20 minutes.
2. Carefully pour the seasoned broth into the fondue pot, keeping the liquid at a simmer.
3. Prepare the octopus, cuttlefish, and langoustines, ensuring they are clean and ready to cook. Arrange them suitably on a platter.
4. Guide guests to cook the seafood in the simmering broth: octopus and cuttlefish pieces for 2-3 minutes until fully cooked and langoustines for 3-5 minutes until they turn a bright red color.
5. Offer guests dishes of aioli for a creamy dip and spicy tomato sauce for a kick to accompany the cooked seafood.

Nutrition information:

Nutritional value (for mixed seafood and broth only, excluding dipping sauces): Approximately 180 calories, 24g protein, 4g carbohydrates, 4g fats, 0g fiber, 60mg cholesterol, 520mg sodium, 460mg potassium per serving.

---

"Ocean Trio Spectacle" combines the intriguing textures and flavors of octopus, cuttlefish, and langoustines in a communal pot of fragrant, wine-kissed broth. This fondue dish is a feast for the senses, inviting diners to savor a spread from under the sea, each piece cooked to tender perfection and complemented by bold and bright dipping sauces.

## 5.8. "Dipping Delicacies - Sauces and Sides Supremacy"

What would an encore be without the grand finale? Here we introduce the co-stars of the night—sauces and sides. Whether it's a tangy béarnaise or a zesty cocktail sauce, the right accompaniment can elevate your fondue experience to new heights. Let's whisk together some sauce sensations that will garnish our fondue creations with the perfect complementary flavors. Side dishes will follow to round off the meal with harmonious accompaniments.

## 5.8.1.Recipe 49: "Classic Béarnaise Bliss"

Yield: About 1 cup | Preparation time: 5 minutes | Cooking time: 10 minutes.

Ingredients:

- 2 tablespoons white wine vinegar
- 2 tablespoons dry white wine
- 1 tablespoon shallots, finely chopped
- 1 teaspoon tarragon leaves, chopped, plus more for garnish
- 3 egg yolks
- 1 stick (1/2 cup) unsalted butter, melted and hot
- Salt and fresh ground pepper to taste

Directions:

1. In a small saucepan, combine vinegar, wine, shallots, and tarragon. Simmer on low heat until reduced by half. Strain and let cool.
2. In a medium bowl, whisk the egg yolks. Gradually add the cooled reduction while continuing to whisk.
3. Set the bowl over a pot of gently simmering water without letting the bowl touch the water. Whisk the mixture constantly, gradually adding the melted butter until the sauce thickens.
4. Season with salt and pepper and garnish with additional tarragon leaves. Serve warm with beef or chicken fondue.

Nutrition information:

Nutritional value (per tablespoon): Approximately 70 calories, 0.5g protein, 0.1g carbohydrates, 7.5g fats, 0g fiber, 45mg cholesterol, 2mg sodium, 5mg potassium.

## 5.8.2. Recipe 50: "Zesty Citrus Ponzu Sauce"

Yield: About 1 cup | Preparation time: 5 minutes | Cooking time: 0 minutes.

Ingredients:

- 1/2 cup soy sauce
- 1/4 cup lemon juice
- 1/4 cup orange juice
- 1 tablespoon mirin (sweet rice wine)

- 1 teaspoon lemon zest
- 1 teaspoon orange zest
- 1 small garlic clove, grated
- 1/2 teaspoon grated fresh ginger

Directions:

1. In a bowl, combine all the ingredients and whisk together until well blended.
2. Allow the sauce to sit for at least 30 minutes before serving so the flavors can meld together.
3. Serve with any seafood or Chinoise-style fondue for a tangy, umami-rich dipping experience.

Nutrition information:

Nutritional value (per tablespoon): Approximately 10 calories, 1g protein, 2g carbohydrates, 0g fats, 0g fiber, 0mg cholesterol, 920mg sodium, 35mg potassium.

## 5.8.3. Recipe 51: "Creamy Horseradish Concoction"

Yield: About 1 cup | Preparation time: 5 minutes | Cooking time: 0 minutes.

Ingredients:

- 1/2 cup sour cream
- 2 tablespoons prepared horseradish, drained
- 1 tablespoon Dijon mustard
- 1 teaspoon apple cider vinegar
- 1 tablespoon chives, finely chopped
- Salt and black pepper to taste

Directions:

1. In a mixing bowl, combine the sour cream, horseradish, Dijon mustard, and apple cider vinegar. Stir until well mixed.
2. Add chives, salt, and pepper. Adjust the seasonings to your taste.
3. Chill for at least 1 hour before serving to allow the flavors to develop.
4. Ideal for pairing with beef or game fondue, offering a punchy and refreshing taste contrast.

Nutrition information:

Nutritional value (per tablespoon): Approximately 20 calories, 0.2g protein, 0.9g carbohydrates, 1.5g fats, 0.1g fiber, 4mg cholesterol, 33mg sodium, 20mg potassium.

**Side Dish Recommendations:**

For a well-rounded fondue soirée, serve an array of sides that complement the main event:

- Crusty Artisan Bread: Cubed or torn into bite-sized pieces for dipping. Select a variety such as sourdough, baguette, and rye for texture variety.
- Roasted New Potatoes: Parboiled and then roasted with olive oil, rosemary, and sea salt, they're perfect for snagging with fondue forks and swirling in creamy sauces.
- Steamed Vegetables: Broccoli, asparagus, and cauliflower lightly steamed retain a slight crunch and stand up well to thick sauces.
- Salad Greens: A fresh green salad dressed with a light vinaigrette offers a crisp, refreshing counterpoint to the richness of fondue.
- Pickles and Chutneys: Assorted pickles, chutney, and relish provide a sweet or sour tang to cleanse the palate between bites.

With these sauce creations and side dishes, we ensure every plunge into the fondue pot is met with oomph and every palate leaves satisfied. Enjoy the dipping and the company it brings together!

# Chapter 6: "Cheese Chronicles: Dipping into Tradition"

Welcome to the warm and inviting world of cheese fondue, where melted cheese serves as both a dish and a unifying experience. As we dive spoon-first into Chapter 6, "Cheese Chronicles: Dipping into Tradition," we're about to unravel the golden threads of this beloved culinary masterpiece.

In this chapter, we pay homage to classic cheese fondue foundations. We'll wander through the alpine pastures of Switzerland where fondue is said to have taken its first melty steps, and we'll cross into the charming French regions where each dip of bread brings you closer to the heart of fondue country. With our selection of time-honored recipes, even the first-time fondue enthusiast will become a melted cheese connoisseur.

## 6.1. Classic Cheese Fondue Foundations

The aroma of a good cheese fondue is as intoxicating as its rich history. Whether it's the legendary "moitié-moitié" with its hearty blend of Gruyère and Vacherin or the French fondue Savoyarde laced with Beaufort, Comté, and Emmental, these recipes have whisked fondue lovers away on a delicious journey for centuries.

Without further ado, let's submerge ourselves in some classic recipes.

### 6.1.1. Recipe 52: "Traditional Swiss 'moitié-moitié'"

Yield: 4 servings | Preparation time: 15 minutes | Cooking time: 20 minutes.

Ingredients:

- 200g Gruyère cheese, grated
- 200g Vacherin Fribourgeois cheese, grated
- 1 garlic clove, halved
- 1 cup dry white wine
- 1 teaspoon lemon juice
- 1 tablespoon cornstarch
- 1 tablespoon kirsch (cherry brandy)
- Freshly ground nutmeg and pepper to taste
- Cubed French bread for dipping

Directions:

1. Rub the inside of the fondue pot with the halves of garlic, then discard.
2. Pour the white wine and lemon juice into the pot and heat gently until hot, but not boiling.
3. In a bowl, blend the cornstarch with the kirsch to create a slurry.
4. Gradually add the cheese to the pot, stirring constantly in a zig-zag pattern (not a circle) to prevent the cheese from balling up.
5. Once the cheese melts and starts to bubble gently, stir in the cornstarch slurry to thicken the fondue.
6. Season with nutmeg and pepper, then serve with cubed bread.

Nutrition information:

Nutritional value: Approximately 650 calories, 35g protein, 5g carbohydrates, 30g fats, 0g fiber, 100mg cholesterol, 400mg sodium, 100mg potassium per serving.

### 6.1.2. Recipe 53: "Fondue Savoyarde"

Yield: 4 servings | Preparation time: 15 minutes | Cooking time: 20 minutes.

Ingredients:

- 150g Beaufort cheese, grated
- 150g Comté cheese, grated
- 150g Emmental cheese, grated
- 1 garlic clove, halved
- 1 cup dry white wine

- 2 teaspoons lemon juice
- 1 tablespoon cornstarch
- 2 tablespoons dry sherry
- A pinch of paprika
- Cubed crusty bread, for dipping

Directions:

1. Rub the fondue pot with the garlic halves, then discard them.
2. Combine the wine and lemon juice in the pot, warming over medium heat until hot.
3. Mix the cornstarch with the sherry to create a smooth blend.
4. Gradually add the trio of cheeses to the wine, stirring consistently until melted and creamy.
5. Once bubbling, incorporate the cornstarch mix and stir until the fondue fully thickens.
6. Season with a pinch of paprika and serve with the bread for dipping.

Nutrition information:

Nutritional value: Approximately 620 calories, 32g protein, 5g carbohydrates, 28g fats, 0g fiber, 90mg cholesterol, 300mg sodium, 90mg potassium per serving.

## 6.1.3. Recipe 54: "Gruyère and Garlic Fondue"

Yield: 4 servings | Preparation time: 15 minutes | Cooking time: 15 minutes.

Ingredients:

- 400g Gruyère cheese, grated
- 2 garlic cloves, minced
- 1 cup dry white wine
- 1 tablespoon flour
- 1 tablespoon lemon juice
- A pinch of cayenne pepper
- Fresh parsley, finely chopped for garnish
- Assorted vegetables and cubed French bread for dipping

Directions:

1. Over medium heat, warm the wine and lemon juice in the fondue pot.
2. Toss the grated Gruyère with flour to coat.
3. Add the garlic to the wine, followed by the Gruyère cheese, stirring until the cheese is melted and smooth.
4. Add a pinch of cayenne pepper, adjusting to taste.

5. Serve garnished with fresh parsley and alongside a platter of assorted vegetables and bread.

Nutrition information:

Nutritional value: Approximately 610 calories, 30g protein, 6g carbohydrates, 29g fats, 0g fiber, 90mg cholesterol, 350mg sodium, 80mg potassium per serving.

---

These foundational recipes are just the beginning. Let's raise our fondue forks to the classics as we prepare to branch out to global and modern takes on this sumptuous dish. With these foundations, you're well-equipped to host a night of international camaraderie centred around the bubbling pot of cheese.

As the audience savors the traditions, let's whisk in a few more timeless recipes that have gathered friends and kin around the crackling hearth of fondue pots for generations.

## 6.1.4. Recipe 55: "Alpine Cheese Delight"

Yield: 4 servings | Preparation time: 15 minutes | Cooking time: 15 minutes.

Ingredients:

- 200g Raclette cheese, grated
- 200g Appenzeller cheese, grated
- 1 garlic clove, minced
- 1 cup dry white wine
- 1 teaspoon lemon juice
- 1 tablespoon cornstarch
- 2 tablespoons kirsch or pear brandy
- A pinch of ground white pepper
- A small grate of nutmeg
- Cubed pumpernickel and sourdough for dipping

Directions:

1. Begin by combining the white wine and lemon juice in the fondue pot. Warm them gently over medium heat without bringing them to a boil.
2. Mix the cornstarch with the kirsch to create a smooth slurry.
3. Add the minced garlic to the pot, then gradually stir in the grated Raclette and Appenzeller cheese until completely melted and smooth.
4. Whisk in the cornstarch slurry to thicken the fondue to a velvety consistency.
5. Season with white pepper and a touch of nutmeg, then serve with the cubed pumpernickel and sourdough bread.

Nutrition information:

Nutritional value: Approximately 630 calories, 34g protein, 5g carbohydrates, 32g fats, 0g fiber, 97mg cholesterol, 370mg sodium, 95mg potassium per serving.

## 6.1.5. Recipe 56: "Cheddar and Beer Fondue Fusion"

Yield: 4 servings | Preparation time: 10 minutes | Cooking time: 20 minutes.

Ingredients:

- 300g sharp Cheddar cheese, grated
- 100g Gouda cheese, grated
- 1 cup light beer (such as a pilsner or lager)
- 1 garlic clove, minced
- 1 tablespoon all-purpose flour
- 1 tablespoon Worcestershire sauce
- 1 teaspoon dry mustard powder
- Freshly ground black pepper, to taste
- Cubed pretzels and fresh apple slices for dipping

Directions:

1. Coat the grated Cheddar and Gouda cheeses with flour in a bowl.
2. In your fondue pot, heat the beer and minced garlic over medium heat until steaming but not boiling.
3. Gradually add the floured cheeses to the pot, stirring continuously until melted and combined into a creamy mixture.
4. Stir in the Worcestershire sauce and dry mustard powder.
5. Season with black pepper, and serve with a mixture of cubed pretzels and apple slices for a comforting and heartwarming fondue take.

Nutrition information:

Nutritional value: Approximately 520 calories, 28g protein, 15g carbohydrates, 36g fats, 0g fiber, 85mg cholesterol, 590mg sodium, 120mg potassium per serving.

## 6.1.6. Recipe 57: "Fontina Fonduta with Truffle Oil"

Yield: 4 servings | Preparation time: 10 minutes | Cooking time: 15 minutes.

Ingredients:

- 400g Fontina cheese, diced
- 1 cup heavy cream
- 2 egg yolks
- 2 tablespoons truffle oil
- Salt, to taste

61

- Chopped chives and freshly ground black pepper for garnish
- Assorted vegetables (like blanched broccoli, roasted mushrooms, and mini potatoes) for dipping

Directions:

1. In a fondue pot, heat the heavy cream over medium heat until it begins to bubble around the edges.
2. Reduce the heat to low and add the diced Fontina cheese, stirring until the cheese is melted and the mixture smooths.
3. Beat the egg yolks in a small bowl, and then add a spoonful of the hot cheese mixture to temper the yolks.
4. Gradually stir the tempered yolks back into the cheese fondue, stirring constantly until creamy.
5. Drizzle in the truffle oil and season with salt, adjusting to your taste.
6. Serve garnished with chopped chives and freshly ground black pepper, accompanied by an array of vegetables for dipping.

Nutrition information:

Nutritional value: Approximately 600 calories, 25g protein, 4g carbohydrates, 52g fats, 0g fiber, 270mg cholesterol, 620mg sodium, 90mg potassium per serving.

## 6.1.7. Recipe 58: "Champagne and Swiss Cheese Celebration"

Yield: 4 servings | Preparation time: 15 minutes | Cooking time: 25 minutes.

Ingredients:

- 200g Emmental cheese, grated
- 200g Gruyère cheese, grated
- 1 shallot, finely chopped
- 1 cup Champagne or sparkling wine
- 1 teaspoon lemon juice
- 1 tablespoon cornstarch
- 1 tablespoon brandy
- A pinch of white pepper and cayenne
- Cubed French baguette, roasted Brussels sprouts, and pear slices for dipping

Directions:

1. In your fondue pot, sauté the shallot in a bit of butter until translucent.
2. Add the Champagne and lemon juice to the pot, heating them gently to a simmer.
3. Toss the cheeses with cornstarch in a bowl before adding them to the pot, stirring until completely melted and creamy.

4. Stir in the brandy and season with white pepper and cayenne.
5. Serve the fondue with an array of French baguette cubes, roasted Brussels sprouts, and pear slices, creating a bubbly fête of flavors for your guests to savor.

Nutrition information:

Nutritional value: Approximately 640 calories, 31g protein, 6g carbohydrates, 33g fats, 0g fiber, 105mg cholesterol, 400mg sodium, 88mg potassium per serving.

---

These recipes anchor us in the art of fondue that has embraced the convivial spirit of communal dining for ages. Stay tuned as we dip our forks into the next part of this cheesy voyage, exploring global twists and modern creations.

# 6.2. Cheese Fondue Around the World

Embark on a global cheese tour without leaving your kitchen as we explore "Cheese Fondue Around the World"! We'll savor the variety of flavors that different cultures bring to the fondue pot. From the creamy Italian Fonduta to the robust British Stilton pot, each recipe is a passport to a delicious destination.

## 6.2.1. Recipe 59: "Italian Fonduta with Truffles"

Yield: 4 servings | Preparation time: 10 minutes | Cooking time: 10 minutes.

Ingredients:

- 300g Fontina Val d'Aosta cheese, cubed
- 1 cup whole milk
- 3 large egg yolks
- 2 tablespoons white truffle oil
- Salt and freshly ground black pepper to taste
- 1 black truffle, shaved (optional)
- Cubed focaccia and blanched asparagus for dipping

Directions:

1. In a bowl, soak the Fontina cheese cubes in milk for about an hour.
2. Transfer the cheese and milk into a fondue pot and melt the cheese over low heat, stirring frequently until smooth.
3. In a separate bowl, beat the egg yolks, then add a few tablespoons of the hot cheese mixture to temper.

4. Slowly pour the egg yolk mixture into the fondue pot, stirring rapidly to incorporate without curdling.
5. Stir in the truffle oil, season with salt and pepper, and continue to cook until the fondue thickens slightly.
6. Serve hot, garnished with shaved truffle (if using) alongside cubed focaccia and blanched asparagus.

Nutrition information:

Nutritional value: Approximately 330 calories, 19g protein, 5g carbohydrates, 26g fats, 0g fiber, 220mg cholesterol, 300mg sodium, 100mg potassium per serving.

## 6.2.2. Recipe 60: "Classic British Stilton Pot"

Yield: 4 servings | Preparation time: 5 minutes | Cooking time: 20 minutes.

Ingredients:

- 200g Stilton cheese, crumbled
- 200g English Cheddar, grated
- 1 cup stout beer (such as Guinness)
- 1 clove garlic, minced
- 1 teaspoon Worcestershire sauce
- A pinch of dry mustard
- Cubed crusty brown bread and green apple slices for dipping

Directions:

1. Gently warm the stout beer in the fondue pot with the minced garlic.
2. Gradually add in Stilton and Cheddar cheeses, stirring until melted and the mixture is smooth.
3. Add Worcestershire sauce and dry mustard. Continue to cook, stirring until all ingredients are well combined and the fondue is velvety.
4. Serve with brown bread and crisp apple slices for a true taste of Britain.

Nutrition information:

Nutritional value: Approximately 400 calories, 21g protein, 7g carbohydrates, 30g fats, 0g fiber, 70mg cholesterol, 520mg sodium, 130mg potassium per serving.

## 6.2.3. Recipe 61: "Mexican Queso Fundido"

Yield: 4 servings | Preparation time: 5 minutes | Cooking time: 10 minutes.

Ingredients:

- 200g Oaxaca cheese, shredded

- 200g Monterey Jack cheese, shredded
- 1/2 cup Mexican lager beer
- 1/4 cup pickled jalapeños, chopped
- 1/4 cup tomato, diced
- 1/4 cup onion, finely chopped
- Tortilla chips and fresh tortillas for dipping

Directions:

1. Pour the beer into the fondue pot and heat it over medium until it begins to simmer.
2. Lower the heat and gradually add the shredded cheeses, stirring until completely melted.
3. Once smooth, add jalapeños, tomato, and onion, stirring to combine.
4. Serve the Queso Fundido with a side of tortilla chips and fresh tortillas for a comforting Mexican twist.

Nutrition information:

Nutritional value: Approximately 370 calories, 22g protein, 4g carbohydrates, 29g fats, 0g fiber, 80mg cholesterol, 470mg sodium, 70mg potassium per serving.

## 6.2.4. Recipe 62: "Canadian Cheddar Chalet"

Yield: 4 servings | Preparation time: 5 minutes | Cooking time: 15 minutes.

Ingredients:

- 200g aged Canadian Cheddar, grated
- 200g smoked Gouda, grated
- 1 cup Canadian ale
- 1 clove garlic, minced
- 1 tablespoon maple syrup
- 1 tablespoon cornstarch
- Rye bread cubes and crispy bacon pieces for dipping

Directions:

1. Combine the ale and minced garlic in your fondue pot over medium heat until hot but not boiling.
2. Mix grated cheeses with cornstarch in a separate bowl, then gradually add them into the pot, stirring until the cheeses are fully melted and combined.
3. Drizzle in the maple syrup for a Canadian sweet note, and whisk until the fondue reaches a creamy consistency.
4. Serve the fondue with cubes of rye bread and pieces of crispy bacon for a hearty dipping experience.

Nutrition information:

Nutritional value: Approximately 420 calories, 21g protein, 5g carbohydrates, 34g fats, 0g fiber, 100mg cholesterol, 570mg sodium, 75mg potassium per serving.

Europe has a rich history of cheese fondues, each with unique regional touches that have made them popular. Here are a few recipes that highlight this European love affair with melted cheese.

## 6.2.5. Recipe 63: "Alsatian Munster Melt"

Yield: 4 servings | Preparation time: 10 minutes | Cooking time: 15 minutes.

Ingredients:

- 300g Munster cheese, rind removed and sliced
- 200g Gruyère cheese, grated
- 1 cup Alsatian Riesling
- 1 tablespoon flour
- 1 clove garlic, halved
- A pinch of caraway seeds
- 1 tablespoon Kirsch
- Salt and freshly ground black pepper to taste
- Crusty French bread and boiled potatoes for dipping

Directions:

1. Rub the inside of the fondue pot with the halved garlic clove.
2. Over medium heat, warm up the Riesling in the fondue pot. Do not boil.
3. Toss the sliced Munster and grated Gruyère with flour in a bowl.
4. Gradually add the cheese to the wine in the fondue pot, stirring continuously.
5. Once fully melted, season with caraway seeds, salt, and pepper.
6. Stir in the Kirsch just before serving.
7. Serve with cubes of crusty bread and boiled potatoes for a hearty dip into this Alsatian classic.

Nutrition information:

Nutritional value: Approximately 640 calories, 27g protein, 5g carbohydrates, 48g fats, 0g fiber, 105mg cholesterol, 680mg sodium, 100mg potassium per serving.

## 6.2.6. Recipe 64: "Dutch Edam Dream"

Yield: 4 servings | Preparation time: 15 minutes | Cooking time: 20 minutes.

Ingredients:

- 400g Edam cheese, grated
- 200g Gouda cheese, grated
- 1 cup Dutch beer (pilsner style)
- 2 teaspoons mustard
- 1 clove garlic, minced
- 1 tablespoon cornstarch
- 1 tablespoon water
- Cubed rye bread and apple slices for dipping

Directions:

1. Warm the Dutch beer in the fondue pot and add the minced garlic. Bring it to a low simmer.
2. Mix the cornstarch and water to make a slurry.
3. Slowly incorporate the cheese into the beer, stirring until the cheese completely melts.
4. Add mustard and the cornstarch slurry to the fondue pot, continuing to stir until the fondue is thick and smooth.
5. Serve the Edam-Gouda mixture with traditional Dutch side dips of rye bread and crisp apple slices.

Nutrition information:

Nutritional value: Approximately 570 calories, 26g protein, 6g carbohydrates, 46g fats, 0g fiber, 140mg cholesterol, 950mg sodium, 100mg potassium per serving.

## 6.2.7. Recipe 65: "Catalan Cava Fondue"

Yield: 4 servings | Preparation time: 10 minutes | Cooking time: 15 minutes.

Ingredients:

- 200g Manchego cheese, grated
- 200g Tetilla cheese, grated
- 1 cup Cava
- 1 tablespoon cornstarch
- 1 teaspoon smoked paprika
- 1 baguette, cubed
- Lightly blanched veggies like broccoli or carrots for dipping

Directions:

1. Pour the cava into your fondue pot and heat it gently until it starts to simmer.

2. Mix the cornstarch with a bit of water to create a slurry.
3. Gradually add the Manchego and Tetilla cheeses to the cava, stirring constantly until the cheese is completely melted and incorporated.
4. Add the cornstarch slurry and smoked paprika, and continue to cook, stirring until the fondue is thick and creamy.
5. Serve with traditional Spanish bread and a variety of lightly blanched vegetables, savoring this Catalan-influenced fondue.

Nutrition information:

Nutritional value: Approximately 500 calories, 28g protein, 15g carbohydrates, 35g fats, 1g fiber, 90mg cholesterol, 730mg sodium, 90mg potassium per serving.

## 6.2.8. Recipe 66: "Greek Feta Fondue"

Yield: 4 servings | Preparation time: 10 minutes | Cooking time: 10 minutes.

Ingredients:

- 200g feta cheese, crumbled
- 200g cream cheese
- 1/2 cup milk
- 1 tablespoon lemon juice
- 2 tablespoons fresh oregano, chopped
- A pinch of crushed red pepper flakes
- Pita bread, cucumber slices, and Kalamata olives for dipping

Directions:

1. Mix feta and cream cheese in the fondue pot over medium heat until cheeses start to melt.
2. Whisk in the milk and lemon juice, stirring until the mixture is creamy and smooth.
3. Stir in the fresh oregano and crushed red pepper flakes.
4. Serve with warm pita bread, cucumber slices, and Kalamata olives for a Grecian twist to the fondue classic.

Nutrition information:

Nutritional value: Approximately 320 calories, 12g protein, 7g carbohydrates, 27g fats, 0g fiber, 88mg cholesterol, 670mg sodium, 70mg potassium per serving.

These European fondue recipes encapsulate the essence of their respective regions while offering a cozy and unifying dining experience. Get ready to travel the continent bite by bite, capturing the spirit of each country in your fondue pot.

Certainly, let's explore the hearty and comforting flavors of Eastern Europe and their interpretation of cheese fondue.

## 6.2.9. Recipe 67: "Balkan Kajmak Kettle"

Yield: 4 servings | Preparation time: 10 minutes | Cooking time: 15 minutes.

Ingredients:

- 200g Kajmak or clotted cream
- 200g Kashkaval cheese, grated
- 1/2 cup robust red wine, such as a local Balkan variety
- 1 clove garlic, minced
- 1 tablespoon ajvar (red pepper spread)
- 1 teaspoon paprika
- Salt to taste
- Cubed crusty bread and roasted red peppers for dipping

Directions:

1. Gently heat the red wine in the fondue pot, then add the minced garlic.
2. Stir in the Kajmak or clotted cream until it begins to melt.
3. Gradually add the grated Kashkaval cheese to the pot, stirring until smooth.
4. Once the cheese mixture is creamy, mix in the ajvar and paprika. Add salt to taste.
5. Serve the fondue with cubed crusty bread and roasted red peppers for a dip into the rich flavors of the Balkans.

Nutrition information:

Nutritional value: Approximately 530 calories, 19g protein, 5g carbohydrates, 43g fats, 0g fiber, 110mg cholesterol, 710mg sodium, 80mg potassium per serving.

## 6.2.10. Recipe 68: "Polish Smoked Oscypek Dip"

Yield: 4 servings | Preparation time: 10 minutes | Cooking time: 20 minutes.

Ingredients:

- 200g Oscypek or smoked sheep's milk cheese, grated
- 200g cream cheese
- 3/4 cup light beer, preferably Polish

- 2 teaspoons horseradish, grated
- 1 teaspoon Dijon mustard
- Cubed black bread (such as pumpernickel) and apple slices for dipping

Directions:

1. In the fondue pot, combine the light beer and cream cheese, warming slowly until the cheese melts.
2. Add in the grated oscypek cheese gradually, continuously stirring until the mixture is uniform.
3. Mix in the horseradish and mustard for a sharp, tangy depth to the smoky flavor.
4. Serve hot with the black bread and apple slices for a unique Polish twist on fondue.

Nutrition information:

Nutritional value: Approximately 490 calories, 18g protein, 8g carbohydrates, 39g fats, 0g fiber, 105mg cholesterol, 650mg sodium, 90mg potassium per serving.

## 6.2.11. Recipe 69: "Carpathian Cauldron"

Yield: 4 servings | Preparation time: 10 minutes | Cooking time: 20 minutes.

Ingredients:

- 200g Bryndza (Eastern European sheep's milk cheese), crumbled
- 200g smoked cheese (like Smoked Gouda), grated
- 1 cup chicken broth or light vegetable broth
- 2 tablespoons sour cream
- 1 small onion, finely grated
- Fresh dill, chopped for garnish
- Boiled baby potatoes and crispy bacon bits for dipping

Directions:

1. Warm chicken or vegetable broth in the fondue pot over medium heat.
2. Stir in the sour cream and the finely grated onion, cooking until the onion is soft.
3. Gradually add the crumbled Bryndza and grated smoked cheese, stirring until the cheeses are fully melted and combined.
4. Top with freshly chopped dill just before serving.
5. Perfect as a dip for baby potatoes and sprinkled with crispy bacon, capturing the comforting flavors of the Carpathian region.

Nutrition information:

Nutritional value: Approximately 480 calories, 22g protein, 9g carbohydrates, 39g fats, 0g fiber, 105mg cholesterol, 810mg sodium, 60mg potassium per serving.

---

Hinting at the pastoral traditions and smoked flavors of Eastern European cuisine, these fondue dishes bring warmth and robust taste to any gathering. They embody the comfort of a mountain retreat and the delight of shared meals.

Cheese fondue may not be the first dish that comes to mind when thinking of Central America, the Caribbean, and South America, but these regions' diverse culinary cultures and love for cheese have inspired their own spins on the classic fondue. Let's delve into some recipes that capture the essence of these vibrant regions.

## 6.2.12. Recipe 70: "Caribbean Jerk Cheese Pot"

Yield: 4 servings | Preparation time: 10 minutes | Cooking time: 20 minutes.

Ingredients:

- 200g Pepper Jack cheese, grated
- 200g Mozzarella cheese, grated
- 1 cup coconut milk
- 2 tablespoons jerk seasoning paste
- 1 tablespoon lime juice
- A pinch of cayenne pepper
- Salt to taste
- Cubed pineapple and fried plantains for dipping

Directions:

1. Heat coconut milk in the fondue pot over medium heat until it begins to steam.
2. Add in the jerk seasoning paste and lime juice, stirring to combine.
3. Gradually mix in the Pepper Jack and Mozzarella cheeses until fully melted and the fondue is smooth.
4. Stir in cayenne pepper, and season with salt as required.
5. Serve the fondue with cubed pineapple and fried plantains for a sweet and spicy take on the tropical flavors of the Caribbean.

Nutrition information:

Nutritional value: Approximately 500 calories, 25g protein, 13g carbohydrates, 39g fats, 1g fiber, 80mg cholesterol, 750mg sodium, 200mg potassium per serving.

## 6.2.13. Recipe 71: "South American Chimichurri Cheese Dip"

Yield: 4 servings | Preparation time: 15 minutes | Cooking time: 10 minutes.

Ingredients:

- 200g Queso Fresco, crumbled
- 200g Añejo cheese, grated
- 1 cup whole milk
- 3 tablespoons chimichurri sauce
- 1/2 teaspoon chili flakes
- Fresh cilantro, finely chopped for garnish
- Crusty bread and chorizo slices for dipping

Directions:

1. Warm up the milk in the fondue pot over medium heat, but do not boil.
2. Gradually add in the Queso Fresco and Añejo cheese, stirring until melted and evenly combined.
3. Mix in the chimichurri sauce and chili flakes, blending until you have a smooth texture.
4. Garnish with fresh cilantro upon serving.
5. Offer crusty pieces of bread and spicy slices of chorizo as dippers to enjoy with the herbal and tangy flavors of this South American fondue.

Nutrition information:

Nutritional value: Approximately 455 calories, 25g protein, 12g carbohydrates, 34g fats, 0g fiber, 100mg cholesterol, 680mg sodium, 100mg potassium per serving.

## 6.2.14. Recipe 72: "Argentinian Provoleta"

Yield: 4 servings | Preparation time: 5 minutes | Cooking time: 15 minutes.

Ingredients:

- 400g Provolone cheese, thickly sliced
- 1/4 cup dry red wine
- 1 teaspoon dried oregano
- 1/2 teaspoon red pepper flakes
- 2 tablespoons chimichurri sauce (for topping)
- Crusty bread and assorted olives for dipping

Directions:

1. Place the thick slices of Provolone at the bottom of the fondue pot.
2. Slowly pour the red wine over the cheese.
3. Sprinkle the dried oregano and red pepper flakes evenly over the top.
4. Heat the fondue pot over medium heat, allowing the Provolone to melt and slightly brown at the edges without stirring.

5. Once melted, drizzle the top with chimichurri sauce.
6. Serve straight from the pot with crusty bread and olives to complement the robust flavor of this Argentinian-inspired cheese dish.

Nutrition information:

Nutritional value: Approximately 430 calories, 27g protein, 4g carbohydrates, 33g fats, 0g fiber, 95mg cholesterol, 760mg sodium, 50mg potassium per serving.

---

These fondue variations take the European classic and infuse it with the vibrant, bold flavors characteristic of Central America, the Caribbean, and South America. Enjoy these warm, cheesy dips reminiscent of sunny climates and rich local traditions.

Mexican cuisine offers an array of flavors that can make cheese fondue exciting and unique. Using traditional Mexican cheeses and iconic flavors, these recipes will bring a fiesta to the fondue pot.

## 6.2.15. Recipe 73: "Mexican Fiesta Fondue"

Yield: 4 servings | Preparation time: 10 minutes | Cooking time: 15 minutes.

Ingredients:

- 200g Chihuahua cheese, grated
- 200g Asadero cheese, grated
- 1 cup Mexican beer (like a light lager)
- 2 tablespoons tomato salsa
- 1 fresh jalapeño, seeded and minced
- 1 teaspoon ground cumin
- 1/4 teaspoon smoked paprika
- Salt to taste
- Fresh cilantro, chopped
- Tortilla chips, bread cubes, and raw vegetables for dipping

Directions:

1. Pour the beer into the fondue pot and heat gently until hot, but not boiling.
2. Slowly add the cheeses to the pot, stirring until they're completely melted.
3. Stir in the salsa, minced jalapeño, cumin, and paprika until well combined and smooth. Season with salt as needed.
4. Garnish with fresh cilantro just before serving.
5. Accompany with tortilla chips, bread cubes, and a selection of raw vegetables for dipping.

Nutrition information:

Nutritional value: Approximately 420 calories, 22g protein, 5g carbohydrates, 34g fats, 1g fiber, 89mg cholesterol, 710mg sodium, 120mg potassium per serving.

### 6.2.16. Recipe 74: "Tequila & Lime Queso Fundido"

Yield: 4 servings | Preparation time: 10 minutes | Cooking time: 15 minutes.

Ingredients:

- 200g Monterey Jack cheese, grated
- 200g Queso Quesadilla cheese, grated
- 1/4 cup tequila
- Juice and zest from 1 lime
- 1 small Roma tomato, diced
- 1/4 cup red onion, finely chopped
- 1/4 teaspoon chili powder
- Warm flour tortillas and tortilla chips for dipping

Directions:

1. Combine the tequila and lime juice in the fondue pot, warming the mixture over medium heat.
2. Gradually add in the grated cheeses while continually stirring until the mixture is smooth and fully melted.
3. Mix in the lime zest, diced tomato, chopped red onion, and chili powder, stirring to distribute throughout the fondue.
4. Once all elements are well incorporated, serve hot with warm flour tortillas and tortilla chips for a zesty, Mexican twist.

Nutrition information:

Nutritional value: Approximately 460 calories, 28g protein, 6g carbohydrates, 36g fats, 0g fiber, 100mg cholesterol, 740mg sodium, 90mg potassium per serving.

### 6.2.17. Recipe 75: "Chipotle Chorizo Cheese Dip"

Yield: 4 servings | Preparation time: 10 minutes | Cooking time: 20 minutes.

Ingredients:

- 200g Manchego cheese, grated
- 100g Mexican chorizo, cooked and crumbled
- 1 can (4 oz) chipotle peppers in adobo sauce, finely chopped
- 3/4 cup milk
- 1 tablespoon flour
- Salt to taste

- Warm soft corn tortillas and vegetable sticks for dipping

Directions:

1. In a fondue pot, combine the milk and flour, whisking until smooth before heating.
2. Cook over medium heat, stirring constantly until the mixture begins to thicken.
3. Add the grated Manchego cheese to the pot gradually, stirring until melted and smooth.
4. Stir in the cooked chorizo and chipotle peppers until the mixture is uniformly combined. Season with salt to taste.
5. Serve hot, offering a smoky, spicy cheese dip with warm soft corn tortillas and an array of vegetable sticks for a full Mexican experience.

Nutrition information:

Nutritional value: Approximately 450 calories, 24g protein, 8g carbohydrates, 36g fats, 0.5g fiber, 90mg cholesterol, 830mg sodium, 70mg potassium per serving.

---

These Mexican-inspired fondue ideas are perfect for those who love a little kick of heat with their cheese and enjoy the rich flavors of traditional Mexican cuisine. With each dip, these cheese fondues will transport your taste buds to a vibrant street market under the warm Mexican sun.

---

Let these international cheese fondue recipes carry your taste buds across oceans and continents, and savor how cheese can unite us all with every heartwarming dip. Stay tuned as the next leg of our fondue journey takes us into the age of modern melts, where the classics are given a contemporary twist.

## 6.3. "Modern Melts: The Art of Cheesy Innovation"

As we step into the invitingly warm aura of "Modern Melts," we embrace the innovative spirit of the fondue world. Gone are the days when fondue was constrained by the traditional bounds of Gruyère and Emmental. Today's cheese fondue has ventured into uncharted territory, pairing bold and unconventional flavors to create avant-garde blends that tantalize the palate and excite the senses. Imagine the tang of blue cheese melting into the sweetness of figs, or the smokiness of Gouda mingling with a robust lager. These are the contemporary strokes of genius that redefine what fondue can be.

Let's indulge in recipes that break the mold, daring to pair the unpickable, blend the unblendable, and transform the traditional into the extraordinary. Welcome to the future of fondue – where every pot is a canvas and every cheese a potential masterpiece.

## 6.3.1. Recipe 76: "Blue Cheese and Fig Fusion"

Yield: 4 servings | Preparation time: 10 minutes | Cooking time: 10 minutes.

Ingredients:

- 150g blue cheese, crumbled
- 150g cream cheese, softened
- 1/2 cup dried figs, finely chopped
- 1/2 cup milk
- 1/4 cup port wine
- 1 teaspoon fresh thyme, chopped
- Honey for drizzling
- Walnut bread and sliced pears for dipping

Directions:

1. In your fondue pot, gently warm the milk and port wine over a medium heat.
2. Add in the cream cheese and blue cheese, stirring until the cheeses melt into a rich, smooth base.
3. Stir the finely chopped figs and thyme into the melted cheese mixture, heating through until bubbling gently.
4. Before serving, drizzle with a touch of honey for a balance of sweet and savory.
5. Offer freshly toasted slices of walnut bread and crisp pear slices to complement the complex flavors of this modern melt.

Nutrition information:

Nutritional value: Approximately 380 calories, 14g protein, 20g carbohydrates, 25g fats, 2g fiber, 75mg cholesterol, 680mg sodium, 200mg potassium per serving.

## 6.3.2. Recipe 77: "Smoked Gouda Lager Luxe"

Yield: 4 servings | Preparation time: 10 minutes | Cooking time: 15 minutes.

Ingredients:

- 200g smoked Gouda, grated
- 200g sharp Cheddar, grated
- 1 cup lager beer
- 1 tablespoon unsalted butter
- 1 tablespoon all-purpose flour

- 1 teaspoon Dijon mustard
- 1 teaspoon Worcestershire sauce
- 1/4 teaspoon smoked paprika
- Fresh scallions, chopped for garnish
- Soft pretzels and apple slices for dipping

Directions:

1. Melt the butter in the fondue pot over medium heat and whisk in the flour to create a roux.
2. Pour in the lager beer, stirring constantly until the mixture is smooth and begins to thicken.
3. Gradually add the smoked Gouda and sharp Cheddar, stirring until the cheeses are completely melted.
4. Mix in the Dijon mustard, Worcestershire sauce, and smoked paprika, blending well.
5. Garnish with fresh chopped scallions and serve with soft pretzels and slices of apple, for a dip that's squarely in the modern era but with a nod to tradition.

Nutrition information:

Nutritional value: Approximately 490 calories, 22g protein, 10g carbohydrates, 38g fats, 0g fiber, 100mg cholesterol, 750mg sodium, 150mg potassium per serving.

### 6.3.3. Recipe 78: "Whiskey Cheddar Caramel Dip"

Yield: 4 servings | Preparation time: 5 minutes | Cooking time: 10 minutes.

Ingredients:

- 200g aged Cheddar, shredded
- 2 tablespoons whiskey
- 1/4 cup heavy cream
- 1 tablespoon brown sugar
- 1/2 teaspoon vanilla extract
- A small pinch of sea salt
- Caramel sauce for drizzling
- Granny Smith apple wedges and salted pretzels for dipping

Directions:

1. Combine the whiskey, heavy cream, and brown sugar in a fondue pot and warm over medium heat until the sugar dissolves.
2. Slowly add the shredded Cheddar cheese, constantly stirring until completely melted and smooth.
3. Stir in the vanilla extract and a pinch of sea salt, blending well.

4. Once smooth, drizzle with caramel sauce and stir slightly for a marbled effect.
5. Serve with apple wedges and salted pretzels, creating a fusion of flavors that's uniquely indulgent and quintessentially modern.

Nutrition information:

Nutritional value: Approximately 440 calories, 14g protein, 15g carbohydrates, 33g fats, 0g fiber, 85mg cholesterol, 620mg sodium, 80mg potassium per serving.

---

As we push the envelope with these modern cheese fondue recipes, remember that the key to innovation lies in the balance of flavors. Get creative, be bold, and most importantly, enjoy every cheesy moment of this culinary evolution.

In the modern melting pot, the possibilities are as limitless as your imagination. Let's explore a few more recipes that blend contemporary tastes with the timeless appeal of cheese fondue.

## 6.3.4. Recipe 79: "Harissa Havarti Harmony"

Yield: 4 servings | Preparation time: 10 minutes | Cooking time: 10 minutes.

Ingredients:

- 200g Havarti cheese, grated
- 200g Gruyère cheese, grated
- 1 cup milk
- 2 tablespoons harissa paste
- 1 teaspoon garlic, minced
- 1/4 teaspoon ground cumin
- Roasted vegetable medley and grilled chicken strips for dipping

Directions:

1. Warm the milk in the fondue pot over medium heat until hot but not boiling.
2. Stir in the harissa paste and minced garlic, distributing evenly throughout the milk.
3. Gradually add the grated cheeses to the pot, stirring continuously until melted and smooth.
4. Season with cumin, and adjust for taste.
5. Serve this spicy, creamy concoction with a roasted vegetable medley or grilled chicken strips to dip, creating a harmonious blend of Middle Eastern spice and melty cheese.

Nutrition information:

Nutritional value: Approximately 480 calories, 26g protein, 7g carbohydrates, 38g fats, 1g fiber, 100mg cholesterol, 730mg sodium, 100mg potassium per serving.

### 6.3.5. Recipe 80: "Port Poached Pear and Gorgonzola Pot"

Yield: 4 servings | Preparation time: 15 minutes | Cooking time: 15 minutes.

Ingredients:

- 150g Gorgonzola cheese, crumbled
- 200g Fontina cheese, grated
- 1/2 cup port wine
- 1/2 cup chicken broth
- 1 tablespoon honey
- 1 tablespoon fresh thyme, leaves only
- 2 ripe pears, cored and sliced thin for dipping
- Toasted walnut halves and sourdough cubes for dipping

Directions:

1. In the fondue pot, combine the port wine and chicken broth, and bring to a gentle simmer.
2. Stir in honey and thyme leaves, and continue to warm.
3. Gradually add in the Gorgonzola and Fontina cheeses, stirring constantly until the cheeses melt into a creamy blend.
4. Once the mixture is smooth, serve with thinly sliced port-poached pears, toasted walnut halves, and sourdough bread cubes, creating a symphony of sweet, savory, and aromatic flavors with a touch of refinement.

Nutrition information:

Nutritional value: Approximately 460 calories, 20g protein, 22g carbohydrates, 32g fats, 2g fiber, 80mg cholesterol, 690mg sodium, 150mg potassium per serving.

### 6.3.6. Recipe 81: "Balsamic Fig and Taleggio Cream"

Yield: 4 servings | Preparation time: 15 minutes | Cooking time: 10 minutes.

Ingredients:

- 250g Taleggio cheese, rind removed and cut into small pieces
- 1/4 cup balsamic vinegar reduction
- 1/4 cup fig jam
- 1/2 cup cream
- Fresh rosemary, minced for garnish
- Fresh figs, sliced and assorted charcuterie for dipping

Directions:

1. Over medium heat, warm the cream gently in the fondue pot.
2. Stir in the Taleggio cheese continuously until it melts into a silky consistency.
3. Whisk in the fig jam and balsamic reduction, ensuring they're fully integrated into the cheese.
4. Once the fondue reaches an even, creamy texture, garnish with rosemary.
5. Pair with fresh, ripe fig slices and a selection of charcuterie to enjoy this lusciously sweet and tart fondue pairing that embodies the spirit of modern culinary creativity.

Nutrition information:

Nutritional value: Approximately 510 calories, 18g protein, 25g carbohydrates, 38g fats, 1g fiber, 90mg cholesterol, 800mg sodium, 200mg potassium per serving.

let's continue this delicious rodeo with a few more inventive concoctions that push the boundaries of cheesy bliss.

## 6.3.7. Recipe 82: "Roasted Garlic and Goat Cheese River"

Yield: 4 servings | Preparation time: 15 minutes | Cooking time: 20 minutes.

Ingredients:

- 200g goat cheese, softened
- 100g cream cheese
- 1 head of garlic, roasted and cloves mashed
- 1/2 cup white wine
- 1/4 teaspoon dried thyme
- 1 tablespoon chopped chives
- Salt and freshly cracked black pepper to taste
- Seedless grapes and sliced baguette for dipping

Directions:

1. In the fondue pot, combine the mashed roasted garlic with the white wine and warm over medium heat.
2. Stir in the thyme, chives, and then gradually incorporate the goat cheese and cream cheese until the mixture is smooth.
3. Season with salt and pepper to your liking.
4. Serve this savory fondue with seedless grapes and slices of a fresh baguette to complement the tangy goat cheese and aromatic garlic.

Nutrition information:

Nutritional value: Approximately 380 calories, 18g protein, 12g carbohydrates, 28g fats, 0g fiber, 45mg cholesterol, 460mg sodium, 130mg potassium per serving.

### 6.3.8. Recipe 83: "Pesto Genovese Gush"

Yield: 4 servings | Preparation time: 15 minutes | Cooking time: 10 minutes.

Ingredients:

- 200g mozzarella cheese, shredded
- 100g Parmigiano-Reggiano cheese, grated
- 1/2 cup milk
- 1/4 cup basil pesto
- 1 teaspoon lemon zest
- Pinch of red pepper flakes
- Fresh basil leaves for garnish
- Cherry tomatoes and ciabatta cubes for dipping

Directions:

1. Begin by warming the milk in the fondue pot over medium flame until hot.
2. Gradually whisk in the mozzarella and Parmigiano-Reggiano cheeses until melted and creamy.
3. Stir in the basil pesto, lemon zest, and a pinch of red pepper flakes until evenly distributed.
4. Once the fondue is smooth and vibrant green in color, garnish with fresh basil leaves.
5. Serve with cherry tomatoes and ciabatta cubes, celebrating the classic flavors of Italy with a twist.

Nutrition information:

Nutritional value: Approximately 420 calories, 20g protein, 3g carbohydrates, 36g fats, 0g fiber, 72mg cholesterol, 700mg sodium, 60mg potassium per serving.

### 6.3.9. Recipe 84: "Spicy Kimchi Cheese Cauldron"

Yield: 4 servings | Preparation time: 15 minutes | Cooking time: 15 minutes.

Ingredients:

- 200g sharp white Cheddar cheese, grated
- 100g Gouda cheese, grated
- 3/4 cup full-fat milk
- 1/2 cup quality kimchi, chopped
- 1 tablespoon gochujang (Korean red chili paste)
- 1 teaspoon soy sauce
- 1/2 teaspoon sesame oil

- Sliced green onions for garnish
- Cooked rice cakes (tteok) and steamed broccoli for dipping

Directions:

1. Heat the milk in the fondue pot on medium, bringing it up to a gentle steaming without boiling.
2. Slowly stir in the Cheddar and Gouda cheeses until they're melted and integrated into the milk.
3. Add the chopped kimchi, gochujang, soy sauce, and sesame oil, stirring consistently to ensure a smooth, spicy mixture.
4. Once thoroughly mixed, the fondue should have a slight fiery hue and a bold flavor.
5. Garnish with green onions and serve with chewy rice cakes and steamed broccoli for a Korean-inspired kick.

Nutrition information:

Nutritional value: Approximately 410 calories, 18g protein, 8g carbohydrates, 32g fats, 1g fiber, 90mg cholesterol, 950mg sodium, 200mg potassium per serving.

Each of these modern melt recipes reimagines the traditional cheese fondue, infusing it with new life and flavor. They defy expectations, blending the familiar comfort of melted cheese with surprising and bold new partners. Gather your friends, heat your fondue pot, and dip into the future of fondue—one courageous concoction at a time. Enjoy the creative journey!

# 6.4. From Milk to Melt

Alas, the quest for the holy grail of melting cheese begins not in the hallowed halls of a distant past, but quite possibly within the confines of your refrigerator.

Welcome, dear reader and cheese whisperer, to the noble league of the "Cheese Champions," where cheddar is sharp, Gruyère is nutty, and the humble curd is transformed into bubbling pools of ambrosia.

Let's don the helmet of knowledge and pluck the bravest from our cheese battalion; those who melt without fear, blend without prejudice, and emulsify into a battalion of deliciousness.

## Choosing Your Cheese Champions

Without further ado, here are the noble knights of the fondue round table:

### "Sir Slice-a-lot" (The Melting Maestros)

- Gruyère the Great: A Swiss hero; nutty with a hint of sweetness, and melts like a dream.
- Emmental the Even-Tempered: With holes as grand as its flavor, it pairs diplomacy with melt-ability.
- The Fontina Fellowship: A gathering of Italian artisans, mingling tart with cream in a smooth surrender.

### "The Flavorful Fellowship" (The Tasters and Terroirs)

- Cheddar the Sharp: Brooding with intensity, its age brings a tang worthy of any pot.
- Comté the Complex: Gifting the fondue its rich, nutty complexity from the lush hills of France.

### "The Silky Path" (The Texture Tacticians)

- Mozzarella the Mellow: Often stringy in nature, best left to pizzas and knightly quests of caprese.
- Monterey Jack the Jovial: A mild companion offering superb melting without theatrics.

### "The Exotic Envoys" (Exciting Alternatives)

- The Halloumi Order: Grilled to perfection but in fondue, often remains aloof and unyielding.
- The Soft Cheese Squires: Brie and Camembert, creamy in pursuit but can be a wild card in the fondue pot.

### "The Art of Substitution" (Master of Cheese Disguise)

- No Gruyère in your garrison? Fear not! Muster the Jarlsberg or the Swiss for a similar flavor.
- Desired Fontina absent? Call forth Provolone or young Asiago to enter the melty fray.

Armed with this knowledge, may your fondue be successful and your cheese never flee its post. The melting pot awaits, my dairy-devoted companion, for we have cheese to conquer and taste buds to win!

Onward to the pot!

**"The Perfect Pairing and Blending Guide"**

In "The Perfect Pairing and Blending Guide," we'll cultivate the artistry behind crafting the quintessential fondue blend. Just as a maestro conducts an orchestra to create harmony, so too must we conduct our cheeses to achieve fondue nirvana.

**Fondue Harmony: A Cheese Symphony**

Imagine each cheese as an instrument; the milky mozzarella is the cello—mellow, the piquant blue cheese, the piccolo—sharp and noticeable. To create harmony in our fondue pot, we blend the voices of our cheese ensemble to achieve the perfect pitch of taste and texture.

**The Cheese Triad: Base, Enhancer, and Accent**

- Base Cheese: This cheese forms the creamy backdrop of your fondue. Think of Fontina, a cheese that melts with ease and sets the stage with its creamy consistency. Without the base, your fondue may lack foundation.
- Enhancer Cheese: The supporting role that amplifies the fondue with depth and complexity. Gruyère is our enhancer, lending a nutty, slightly sweet dimension. The enhancer is the flavor friend that says, "Trust me, you need this."
- Accent Cheese: This is your fondue's flourish, the bold pop of blue cheese or the tang of a sharp Cheddar that makes your taste buds do a double-take. Accent cheese is the cameo appearance everyone talks about after the show.

**Cheese Blending Principles**

- Ratio Rule: A tried and true ratio to begin with is 50% base, 30% enhancer, and 20% accent. This ensures a balance where no single cheese overpowers the harmony.
- Texture Tango: When combining cheeses, aim for a mix that collectively leans into creaminess. Hard and semi-hard cheeses that yield to the warmth with grace are the dance partners you're looking for.
- Flavor Fusion: Taste your cheeses beforehand. Your base should be mild, your enhancer more flavorful, and your accent the most potent. Together, they should sing a beautiful flavor aria—not battle for a solo.
- Heat Wisely: To meld the trio, heat your fondue gently. Warm your base first—it requires the most coaxing—before introducing the enhancer. The accent is the finishing touch, added just before the final curtain rise, or in this case, service.

**The Cheese Swap Shop**

- No Fontina? Gouda can take the stage.
- Out of Gruyère? Emmental can play the part with aplomb.
- Blue cheese too bold? A milder Roquefort can spread subtle intrigue.

Fear not the experimental stage; the best fondues are often born of daring dalliances in the kitchen. With your lab coat donned and your cheese triad in mind, embark on this gastronomic journey to melting mastery.

### "The Science of Silky Smooth"

Ah, the quest for the silkiest, smoothest cheese fondue is not unlike the alchemist's pursuit for turning ordinary metals into gold. And just like our mystical counterparts, we fondue fanatics have our own set of arcane knowledge and secret incantations (or, as the less romantically inclined might call them, techniques and principles).

So, don your wizard's hat (chef's hat will do as well), and let's dive into the cauldron of fondue making to uncover the scientific spells that create that dreamy, velvety consistency.

### The Dance of the Dairy

Cheese, the star of our show, is primarily composed of fats, proteins, and water. When heat is applied, cheese undergoes a transformation, called melting, but not all cheeses take to this change the same way. The key to achieving smoothness in your fondue is managing these components harmoniously, and a few select ingredients act as the peacekeepers in this volatile dance.

### The Role of Acid

Enter wine and lemon juice—the Dumbledore and Gandalf of the fondue world. These aren't just for flavor; they contain acids that help prevent the cheese proteins from clumping together. They play the crucial role of 'emulsifiers', substances that help mix things together that normally don't mix well (like water and oil, or in this case, cheese and liquid). No lumps, no bumps, just the smooth, creamy fondue we all covet.

### The Majesty of Starch

Cornstarch is another vital player in our fondue potion. When mingled with a splash of alcohol (like kirsch) or your acid-source (the wine), it seals the proteins within the cheese, allowing them to unwind in the heat without becoming a tangled mess that results in clumpiness. Thus, cornstarch acts like a charm, ensuring our melted cheese mixture retains a delightful, dip-worthy texture.

### Alcohol's Two-Faced Nature

A dash of spirits is a common ingredient in many fondue recipes, and not just for the kick it provides. Alcohol lowers the mixture's boiling point, which can help prevent overheating (the bane of smooth fondue), and it helps dissolve the fat-soluble flavor compounds, enhancing the taste and aiding in the melt.

**Stirring the Cauldron**

A complete melt requires consistent heat and gentle stirring—a wooden spoon or spatula making a figure-eight motion across the pot works wonders. This technique ensures an even heat distribution and prevents the proteins from seizing up and separating from the fat.

**The Bewitching Balance**

A successful fondue requires a delicate balancing act. Too much heat, and your cheese will rebel; too little, and it won't join forces with its pot comrades. Keep your fondue at a gentle simmer, where heat waves caress the cheese into sublime submission.

**The Rescue Rituals**

Even the best-laid plans of mice and men often go awry, and so may your fondue. If the pot foretells a gritty future, fear not—the cauldron can still be righted. If you sense separation, remove the pot from the heat. Add a spoonful of lemon juice or more wine and whisk like a sorcerer casting a reversal spell, bringing the fondue back from the brink.

In the world of fondue-making, the science of smoothness is akin to the search for the philosopher's stone - a pursuit of perfection that, with a bit of knowledge and a lot of care, yields rich, delicious rewards. So wield your whisk with wisdom, dear cheese alchemist, and may your fondue always flow like liquid gold.

**Local Loves: Finding Fondue Cheese Near You**

When the craving for fondue hits, it's not always possible to find the traditional stars of the show—like Gruyère or Emmental—especially if you're rustling up a feast in a locale where such delights are as scarce as a snowflake in the Sahara. But do not fear, for the essence of fondue is adaptation and innovation.

**Fondue is Where the Home Is**

- Staple Superstars: Start with what's available. Many regions have their local staple cheeses, be they queso fresco in Mexico or gouda in the Netherlands. These can form the base of your experimental fondue.

**Be Your Own Cheese Detective**

- Taste and Texture: Seek out locals and cheese mongers and ask about cheeses that are melty, flavorful, and perhaps a little stretchy—leave no stone unturned or cheese untasted!
- Go for Gold: Look for local semi-hard cheeses with a good melting property to substitute for Gruyère. A cheese that's pale gold, has a supple texture and melts when held in the warmth of your hand harbors fondue potential.

### Culture and Creaminess

- Cream of the Crop: Higher fat content means creamier fondue, so for your base cheese, opt for something rich and lush from your region—be it triple cream brie or a luscious local camembert.
- Flavor Flares: Cheese is an expression of terroir—so regional varieties offer unique flavors. Think of replacing the nuttiness of Emmental with a nutty local cheese, like Ossau-Iraty from the French Pyrenees or even a creamy Cașcaval from Eastern Europe.

### Fondue Without Borders

- Fondue Fusion: Who says you can't have a fondue that speaks more than one culinary language? Blend a Mexican Oaxaca with a Dutch Edam, or mix a tangy British Cheddar with creamy Italian Fontina.
- Substitution Guide:
  - No Gruyère? Opt for Alpine-style cheeses that offer a similar melting quality and nutty taste.
  - Can't find Vacherin? Look for cheeses with a bloomy rind and rich, creamy interior that melts at a whisper.
  - Emmental elusive? Any medium-firm cheese that grates well and has a slightly sweet, mild flavor can stand in.

### Fondue for the People

- Ask the Experts: Don't be shy to strike up a conversation with local cheese enthusiasts. Share your fondue vision, and they might just have the perfect cheese suggestion for you.

Fondue fans, fear not the unknown. Embrace the cheese journey, and let it take you to delicious destinations you've never before imagined. Armed with a sense of adventure and a love for all things cheesy, you'll soon discover the joy of a fondue that truly speaks the language of your locale.

### Troubleshooting Common Fondue Faux Pas

Even the most experienced fondue forgers can encounter the occasional mishap. The fondue pot is a cauldron of unpredictability, but fear not! Herein lie the ancient secrets to rectify any fondue faux pas you may stumble upon.

### The Curse of the Clumpy Cheese

Should your fondue begin to resemble a stringy web fit for a spider's dinner rather than a smooth sanctuary for bread, it's likely due to the cheese not being at room temperature or the pot being too hot.

The Fix: Remove the pot from the heat and add a splash of acid, be it lemon juice or a tad more wine. Stir gently and slowly, reheating with more care this time.

## The Oil Slick Dilemma

Behold the separation of fat—an unwelcome guest at the fondue table. This occurs when cheese's fat says farewell to the mixture, often due to too much heat.

The Fix: One solution is to whisk a small amount of cornstarch and wine together and slowly stir this into your fondue. It can help reunite the errant fat with the rest of the mixture.

## The Lumpy Potion Problem

Lumps in your fondue can ruin the texture and the enjoyment. Lumps form when cheese is added too quickly or isn't stirred enough.

The Fix: Turn down the heat and whisk vigorously. If it remains lumpy, a quick blitz with an immersion blender can restore the smooth texture you crave.

## The Thin Gravy Snafu

A fondue that's too thin slinks off your dippers, a sad specter of its potential self.

The Fix: You can thicken a watery fondue with extra cheese mixed with flour or cornstarch. Add this gently until you reach the desired consistency.

## The Burnt Bottom Blunder

You've neglected your pot only to find a charred layer of cheese haunting the bottom. This bitter flavor can invade your entire fondue.

The Fix: If you catch it early, you can pour the top, unburned portions into a new pot, leaving the burnt layer behind. Always keep your fondue on the lowest possible heat setting.

## The Hardened Top Travesty

A fondue neglected can form a hard top crust, like a cheese glacier atop your molten lake.

The Fix: Stir it back into the pot gently. To prevent this, keep the fondue covered between servings or maintain a heat that allows the top to bubble slightly.

## The Stiffened Cheese Statue

Perhaps through distraction or debate, your fondue has cooled and stiffened into a sculpture of the Colossus' cheese cousin.

The Fix: Gently reheat your fondue on the stove, stirring continuously to encourage it back to its former riverine glory.

Remember, dear cheese enthusiast, that fondue is as forgiving as it is delicious. With patience, a spoon, and a dash of culinary cunning, almost any fondue foible can be corrected, leaving you with a pot of cheesy perfection ready to be dipped into once more.

**Choosing Your Cheese Champions**

The foundation of any good cheese fondue is, unsurprisingly, the cheese. When selecting your cheeses, consider these key properties:

Melting Ability: Cheeses with higher moisture content and a balance of fats and proteins tend to melt more smoothly. Younger cheeses like Gouda, Fontina, and Monterey Jack are excellent melters.

Flavor Profile: Aim for a mix of mild and sharp cheeses. Harmonize a nutty Gruyère with creamy Emmental for a classic balance. For a sharper taste, add in a bit of aged Cheddar or spicy Pepper Jack.

Texture Considerations: Some cheeses, like Mozzarella, can become stringy when melted, which may be desirable in some dishes but typically not in fondue. For fondue, cheeses that melt evenly, without too many stretchy strands, are preferred.

**Traditional Cheeses and Substitutes:**

- Emmental: A sweet, nutty flavor with smooth melting qualities. Can be substituted with Jarlsberg or young Swiss cheese.
- Gruyère: Balances well with other cheeses, offering a creamy melt. Substitute with Comté or Beaufort.
- Fontina: Brings a mild, slightly tart flavor to the pot. Can be substituted with Taleggio or Provolone.
- Comté: Adds a complex nuttiness; similar substitutes include aged Gruyère or even certain types of aged Cheddar.

Now, let's proceed to blending these champions into a pot of gold.


# 6.5. Dipper's Delight: Beyond the Basic Bread Cube

Welcome to the grand tableau of dippers, where the humble bread cube ascends to join a parade of sumptuous morsels ready to take the plunge into the golden cheesy abyss. We venture beyond the ordinary into a realm of robust flavors and textures, creating a sensorial landscape waiting to be explored, one dip at a time.

**"Meat Maestros"**

For those fond of fondue carne, here are choices fit for a king:

- Charcuterie: Prosciutto, salami, and mortadella, thinly sliced, become riveting when swirled in cheese.
- Meatballs: Miniature, herbed, and cooked to tender perfection, these orbs of delight bring substance to the dip.
- Sausage: Spicy chorizo or herby chicken sausage, grilled and sliced, adds a smoky resonance.
- Chicken Satay: Skewered and grilled with a hint of curry, these are ready for their cheese coating.

**"Vegetable Virtuosos"**

For a fresher note that beckons to the health-conscious:

- Crudités: Think rainbow carrots, blanched asparagus, and endive boats.
- Broccolini: Lightly steamed, with tips ready to soak up the cheesy goodness.
- Mini Potatoes: Boiled until just tender, offer a delightful, earthy contrast.
- Artichokes: Marinated hearts bring a tart dimension that battles beautifully with rich cheese.

**"Fruits & Nuts"**

In the orchard of options, sweet meets savory in a symphony of flavors:

- Apples & Pears: Sliced crisp and fresh, the sweet tartness counterbalances the creamy fondue.
- Grapes: Chilled to burst with juiciness amidst the cheese.
- Dried Fruits: Apricots, figs, and dates, a concentrated sweetness to complement the savory.
- Nuts: Think almonds and walnuts, toasted and tossed into the mix for a crunchy surprise.

**"Bakery and Grains"**

From the baker's hands, these dippers are a carb-lovers dream:

- Pretzel Bites: With their salty crust, they're a steadfast pick.
- Rye Bread: Dark and dense, it stands strong against the molten tide.
- Polenta Cubes: Fried to a golden crust, their soft interior marries well with cheese.
- Bagel Chips: For a twist, these bring a satisfying crunch.

**"Sea Harvest"**

For the seafarer in you, dive into these oceanic treats:

- Shrimp: Cooked and chilled, ready for a cheese bath.
- Crab Cakes: Miniature ones work best, poised perfectly on your fork.
- Lobster Chunks: If you're feeling opulent, let these tender pieces indulge in a cheese dip.

**"The Unexpected"**

And for the adventurous, the unconventional dippers that shine:

- Gnocchi: Delicate, bite-sized potato dumplings, boiled and firm.
- Kimchi: For those who like a twist of tang and a bit of fire.
- Pickles: Cornichons and dill pickles offer an acidic punch.
- Honeycomb: Tiny chunks to be transformed with a warm cheese coating for a divinely sweet and savory combination.

With "Dippers Delight," your fondue soirée transforms into a palette of potential, every dip a different delight, every bite a new narrative. So, stretch forth your skewer and let your imagination and taste buds run wild!

# 6.6. Cheese, Wine, and Beyond: A Connoisseur's Companion

In the grand tapestry of culinary couplings, few dances are as divine as that of cheese with its liquid consort. Let us uncork the wisdom of the ages and pour forth libations that lift our fondue feasts to the realm of rapture.

**Wine: The Cheese's Chosen**

Like a faithful squire to a noble knight, the right wine elevates cheese fondue from mere food to a feast for the senses:

- The Classic Matches: A Swiss Fondue and a Fendant are as timeless as the mountains themselves. For your rich cheeseblends featuring Gruyère, seek out the complement of a crisp, acidic Swiss white wine, or perhaps a Chasselas, which embraces the creamy texture with vivacious verve.
- The Bold Alliance: A heady Chardonnay stands shoulder to shoulder with an assertive fondue that sports blue cheese in its battalion. The robust notes of such wines can cut through the richness with the elegance of a well-forged blade.

- The Sweet Whisperers: Dessert wines like Sauternes or a late-harvest Riesling lend a honeyed touch, a perfect foil to the saltier cheeses like aged Cheddar or the sharp tang of a Fontina.
- Red Wine Rendezvous: Dare to pair a full-bodied red with your fondue. A Pinot Noir will not overpower, but will waltz harmoniously with an earthy, truffled concoction.

**Beer: The Frothy Fête**

Ah, beer—wine's cheerful cousin. Its bubbles and breadth of character make for a merry fondue match:

- The Pale Rider: A golden Pilsner cleanses the palate like a fresh alpine breeze, perfect with a mild cheese blend.
- The Stout Hearted: A dark, creamy stout or porter can stand up to the smoky whispers of a Gouda or Swiss cheese fondue. It's a rich echo to the depth of flavors.

**Non-Alcoholic Nectars**

Fear not, for the absence of alcohol does not leave your fondue forlorn. There are beverages abundant with discretion and grace:

- Sparkling Sodas: Choose a spritzer or a non-alcoholic sparkling grape juice that brings a similar effervescence to the table, clearing the palate with its zesty fizz.
- Tea Pairings: The herbal note of a chamomile can be soothing, while the tannins in a black tea add a drying note akin to wine, balancing the cheesy envelopment.
- Fruit Juices: Apple cider offers a tart, sweet balance while pear nectar provides a gentle, rounded sweetness—both excellent with a multilayered cheese pot.

With "Cheese, Wine, and Beyond," your fondue becomes an overture, each sip and dip an act of the play, a sip from the goblet of Dionysus himself. Choose your potion wisely and let your fondue form a concord of flavors, as epicurean as it is eternal.

# 6.7. Fondue Party Planning: The Perfect Melting Pot of Fun

Ah, the fondue party—the zenith of social gatherings where the cheese flows like lava and conviviality cooks to perfection. To host the ultimate fondue party, one must blend the grace of a ballet director with the precision of a maestro. Here are some tips to ensure your fondue affair is as smooth as the cheese in your pot.

### Setting the Stage

- The Table: Arrange your fondue pot—or pots, if you're hosting a fondue fiesta—in the center of a large table. Ensure the space allows for guests to navigate their skewers without a tangle of arms.
- Seating Arrangement: Think round tables for a more intimate setting where everyone can reach the fondue without jostling elbows. Remember, accessibility is key!
- Lighting: Dim the chandeliers and light some candles to create an ambiance that whispers "cozy chalet" rather than "office cafeteria."

### The Fondue Fleet

Hosting multiple fondue options? Cheese, meat, chocolate—how does one keep the fleet from turning into a culinary armada adrift?

- Heat Sources: Electric fondue pots are your allies, giving you precise control over temperature. If using candles or sterno burners, keep spare fuel at hand—lest the flame of the party sputters.
- Pot Placement: Avoid fondue traffic jams. Space out your pots, perhaps a cheese and a chocolate in opposite table lands, a meaty centerpiece. Ensure guests have clarity on what lies within each cauldron.

### Decor to Devour

- Cheese Theme: Golden hues, wooden cutting boards, rustic bread baskets. Sprinkle some edible flowers for a touch of pastoral elegance.
- Chocolate Theme: Think indulgence—a sprinkle of cocoa on the tables, deep browns, and cream colors to match the dessert decadence.
- Meat Theme: A more robust setting—steak knives at the ready, leather coasters, perhaps a garnish of rosemary sprigs that echo the savory offerings.

### The Interactive Menu

- Dipper Variety: Variety is the spice—and savior—of a fondue party. Offer an array of dippers from the traditional breads and fruits to the unexpected delights of pickled vegetables or spiced meatballs.
- Label Love: Lost in the cheese sea? Fear not. Place delicate labels so guests can navigate the dips and sauces with the confidence of a fondue veteran.

### Fondue Flow

- Start with appetizers—grilled veggies and bread with light dips.
- Progress to the main fondue event—meat or cheese, paired with salad.
- Finish with a sweet note of chocolate fondue, as desserts should be.

**Social Serenade**

- Playlist: Choose music that encourages mellow moods and conversation. Perhaps a live guitar session or that jazz vinyl that's been aging like fine wine.
- Games: Introduce fondue games—a lost piece of bread means you share a tale, or perhaps a serenade.

**Safety in Simmering**

- Placement: Keep your dining area clear of dangling cords or anything that can trip up your guests.
- Tools: Ensure every pot has its designated skewers, forks, and serving spoons.

Remember, at the heart of every fondue party is the shared experience—the warm bubble of friendship that forms over a pot of melted cheese or chocolate. A successful fondue party is measured not in the pots emptying, but in the laughter filling the room, the stories shared, and the memories created.

So, tie on your apron, light those burners, and let the fondue revelry begin!

# 6.8. Fondue Etiquette: The Cheese Communal Commandments

Oh, dearest guests of the molten cheese soirée, before you stands not just a fondue pot but the round table of conviviality, a vessel bearing the very essence of communal dining. Heed these commandments of fondue etiquette to navigate the delightful seas of cheese without faux pas.

**"Thou Shalt Not Double-Dip"**

- As the bread crumb proclaims, "One dip, one bite". The double-dip is a misstep in fondue decorum—a breach most grievous, for it besmirches the purity of the communal pot with a crumbly trail of personal history.

**"Honor Thy Fondue Fork"**

- Behold, your fondue fork is your sword in the battle for cheese-coated delights. Use it to cook and to transfer, but never to eat. Once your dipper is dressed in its cheesy finery, guide it to your plate and use a separate eating utensil to savor the victory.

**"No Swords Crossing"**

- When a multitude of forks enter the fondue fray, let the pot not become a battlefield. Each diner must dip in turn, avoiding the clang of metal and the chaos of entangled skewers.

**"Perform the Swift Swirl"**

- Dip with the grace of a gentle zephyr, not with the fervor of a whirlwind. A gentle turn or a delicate figure-eight beneath the cheese surface will ensure an even coating without disturbing the communal calm.

**"Keep Calm and Carry On Dipping"**

- Should a morsel abandon the fork mid-dip, do not lament. Embrace the age-old tradition of the "fondue challenge"—be it a song, a joke, or perhaps a dance. Perform with mirth and then proceed with your dipping rite anew.

**"Embrace the Fondue Flow"**

- As the molten cheese ebbs and flows, allow conversation to mirror this dance. Fondue is not just a meal; it's a social sculpture, where every dip and swirl adds to the evening's shared memory.

**"The Cheese Pot Is Sacred"**

- Leave not a fortress of crust upon the night's end. The fondue pot is best enjoyed when all guests partake in the creamy indulgence until naught but a silken memory remains.

With these guidelines graven upon your heart, forge forth into the indulgent night, armed with the secrets to fondue bliss. Let your soiree be a melody of merriment, a dance of dippers, and a testament to the ageless allure of cheese fondue. The pot is ready, the etiquette set, the night your canvas—dip, dine, delight!

# 6.9. Cheese Fondue Safety Tips: Melt with Care

As we close the chapter on our cheese fondue saga, let us not forget the sacred scrolls of safety, for a bubbling pot of cheese, while a delight, does come with cautions to heed.

**Heat Safety: Warm Hearts, Not Burnt Hands**

- Steady and Stable: Ensure your fondue set is on a stable surface, well away from table edges. A toppling cauldron of cheese is a tale for tragedy, not for triumph.

- Low and Slow: Cheese fondue must never be rushed. Keep the flame low, as a cheese that's heated too quickly is prone to separation, and more importantly, can burn.

## Serving Sensibly: To Avoid the Scald

- Appropriate Tools: Utilize fondue forks with care. They're designed to transport from pot to plate, not to mouth, and can be quite hot to the touch after a cheese dip.
- Protect Your Paws: Keep a heat-resistant glove or oven mitt handy for when you need to move the pot or adjust the burner.
- Pot Protective: Cheese fondue pots, particularly ceramic ones, can get hot. Always handle with care, and be sure your guests know not to touch the sides of the pot.

## Cheese Cooling Considerations: Preventing the Accidental Cheese Pull

- Monitor the Melt: Keep an eye on the cheese's consistency. If it begins to cool and thicken, a slight increase in heat may be necessary.
- Spatial Awareness: Maintain a clear area around the fondue pot. A pot surrounded by clutter can lead to accidental spills or burns.

## Hygiene Highlights: The Community Pot

- No Double-Dipping: It bears repeating; once a piece has touched your lips, it should not make a subsequent journey into the pot.
- Fresh Forks: For multi-course fondue feasts, starting each course with a clean fork is not just elegant; it's a hygienically sound practice.

## Alcohol Incorporation: A Delicate Splash

- Measures Matter: If your fondue recipe calls for alcohol, measure it out before adding—too much could overpower the dish, too little might not lend the necessary acidity for that smooth texture.
- Fire Foes: When adding alcohol, be sure the fondue pot is away from the burner to eliminate the chance of a flambé surprise. Remember, we're here for the fondue, not fireworks.

With these safety scriptures in mind, may your cheese fondue soirées be nothing short of legendary. Gather around the pot, partake in the palatable pleasantries, and remember—safety is the secret ingredient to ensure your fondue festivities are both joyous and jeopardy-free. Now go forth and fondue with fervor!

# Chapter 7: "Festive Fondue: Recipes for Christmas and New Year"

Grab your fondue forks and gather around the fire, for we're about to embark on a holiday journey that melts the heart as delightfully as cheese in a pot. Welcome to a world where every fondue is a festive celebration, bursting with joy and oozing with the spirit of the season.

## 7.1. A Very Gruyère Christmas

Imagine a Christmas Eve where the snowflakes outside compete with the Gruyère snowflakes melting in your pot. Here are a couple of recipes to start this cozy tradition in your home.

### 7.1.1. Recipe 85: "Midnight Mass Emmental Melt"

Yield: 6 servings | Preparation time: 15 minutes | Cooking time: 20 minutes.

Ingredients:

- 300g Emmental cheese, grated
- 200g Gruyère cheese, grated
- 1 clove garlic, halved
- 1 cup dry white wine (preferably Swiss, like Fendant)
- 1 tbsp lemon juice
- 1 tbsp cornstarch
- 2 tbsp cherry brandy (kirsch)
- A pinch of nutmeg
- Pepper to taste
- Cubed crusty bread, pearl onions, and boiled baby potatoes for dipping

Directions:

1. Rub the inside of your fondue pot with the garlic halves, then discard.
2. Pour the white wine and lemon juice into the pot and heat gently until hot but not boiling.
3. Mix the cornstarch with the kirsch in a bowl to form a smooth slurry.
4. Gradually add the cheese to the wine, stirring constantly until the cheese is fully melted and smooth.
5. Stir in the cornstarch mixture, nutmeg, and pepper, continuing to stir until thickened.
6. Keep the fondue warm as you dip and enjoy with your loved ones after returning from the midnight mass.

Nutrition information:

Nutritional value: Approximately 410 calories, 28g protein, 5g carbohydrates, 29g fats, 0g fiber, 85mg cholesterol, 220mg sodium, 80mg potassium per serving.

### 7.1.2. Recipe 86: "Silent Night, Holy Gruyère Fondue"

Yield: 6 servings | Preparation time: 15 minutes | Cooking time: 20 minutes.

Ingredients:

- 400g aged Gruyère cheese, grated
- 2 tbsp all-purpose flour
- 1 cup apple cider
- 1 tsp Dijon mustard
- 1/4 tsp smoked paprika
- Fresh thyme leaves for garnish
- Sliced apples, roasted Brussels sprouts, and thick cubes of ham for dipping

Directions:

1. Toss the grated Gruyère with flour in a bowl to coat, setting aside.
2. Heat the apple cider in the fondue pot until it begins to simmer.
3. Lower heat and gradually add the cheese mixture, stirring well until melted and smooth.
4. Blend in the Dijon mustard and smoked paprika for a gentle kick.
5. Once the fondue is creamy, garnish it with fresh thyme leaves.
6. Serve with sliced apples, Brussels sprouts, and ham, creating a fondue that's a hymn to the flavors of the holiday season.

Nutrition information:

Nutritional value: Approximately 420 calories, 30g protein, 6g carbohydrates, 31g fats, 0g fiber, 94mg cholesterol, 280mg sodium, 120mg potassium per serving.

---

Stay tuned for more festive recipes to ring in the new year and cherish the old with a fondue pot that's both a source of warmth and a beacon of tradition. May your holidays be merry, your cheese pot bubbly, and every dip bring a sprinkle of yuletide cheer!

## 7.2. The New Year's Eve Bubbly Cheese Pot

As the clock ticks down to a fresh beginning, what better way to usher in the New Year than with a fondue pot that sparkles as brightly as the fireworks in the sky? Let's raise our glasses, or rather, our fondue forks, and celebrate with these effervescent fondue creations that are perfect for your New Year's Eve celebration.

### 7.2.1. Recipe 87: "Champagne Cheddar Cheer"

Yield: 6 servings | Preparation time: 15 minutes | Cooking time: 15 minutes.

Ingredients:

- 200g aged sharp Cheddar, shredded
- 200g Gouda, shredded
- 1 cup Champagne or a good sparkling wine
- 1 shallot, minced
- 1 teaspoon Dijon mustard
- 2 teaspoons cornstarch
- A handful of chives, finely chopped
- A sprinkle of edible gold flakes (optional)
- Cubed brioche, steamed haricots verts, and sliced pear for dipping

Directions:

1. Start by simmering the Champagne and minced shallot in the fondue pot until the mixture reduces slightly.
2. Mix the cornstarch with the cheeses in a separate bowl, ensuring each shred is coated.
3. Gradually incorporate the cheese into the simmering Champagne, stirring constantly until the mixture is smooth.
4. Stir in Dijon mustard for a tangy note.
5. Once ready, sprinkle the concoction with chopped chives and edible gold flakes to ring in the New Year with style.
6. Surround your luminous pot with cubed brioche, crisp haricot verts, and delicate pear slices for a festive culinary countdown.

Nutrition information:

Nutritional value: Approximately 400 calories, 22g protein, 12g carbohydrates, 28g fats, 0g fiber, 80mg cholesterol, 420mg sodium, 125mg potassium per serving.

### 7.2.2. Recipe 88: "Prosecco & Pecorino Pop"

Yield: 6 servings | Preparation time: 15 minutes | Cooking time: 20 minutes.

Ingredients:

- 300g Pecorino Romano, finely grated
- 100g Mascarpone cheese
- 1 cup Prosecco
- 1 clove garlic, halved
- 2 tablespoons apricot preserves

- Fresh thyme for garnish
- Sliced figs, artisanal crackers, and roasted almonds for dipping

Directions:

1. Rub the garlic halves around the inside of the fondue pot, then discard them.
2. Pour in the Prosecco and warm it gently—avoid boiling to keep the sparkle.
3. Whisk in the Mascarpone and Pecorino Romano gradually, stirring continuously for a seamless blend.
4. Once the cheeses have melted and combined, stir in the apricot preserves for a note of sweetness.
5. Garnish with sprigs of fresh thyme just before serving, adding a touch of herbal freshness.
6. Dive into the New Year with a pot surrounded by sweet figs, crunchy crackers, and roasted almonds for a festive celebration of flavor.

Nutrition information:

Nutritional value: Approximately 450 calories, 25g protein, 15g carbohydrates, 34g fats, 0g fiber, 105mg cholesterol, 680mg sodium, 100mg potassium per serving.

---

Welcome the future and say salute to the past with these sparkling cheese pots that embody the spirit of celebration. As you dip into these rich, festive fondues, may they bring with them joy, laughter, and deliciousness to your New Year's Eve. Cheers to a new year of fondue adventures!

# 7.3. Santa's Selection: Cheesy Treats for the Family

Gather 'round, folks of all ages! Here in Santa's cheesy workshop, we've whipped up a selection of fondue treats that the whole family will adore. From the smallest elf to the tallest reindeer in the squad, these recipes are sure to spread cheer, spark smiles, and fill every belly with delight.

### 7.3.1. Recipe 89: "Merry Mozzarella Marvel"

Yield: 6 servings | Preparation time: 10 minutes | Cooking time: 10 minutes.

Ingredients:

- 400g Mozzarella cheese, shredded
- 1 cup whole milk
- 1 tablespoon flour
- 1/2 teaspoon garlic powder
- A pinch of Italian seasoning

- Cubed sourdough bread, cherry tomatoes, and steamed broccoli for dipping

Directions:

1. In a bowl, toss the shredded Mozzarella with flour to coat evenly.
2. Warm the milk in a fondue pot over medium heat—but do not boil.
3. Gradually mix in the Mozzarella, stirring until it is completely melted.
4. Add garlic powder and Italian seasoning for a touch of holiday magic.
5. Serve with sourdough bread, cherry tomatoes, and steamed broccoli, perfect for family members who've been extra good this year.

Nutrition information:

Nutritional value: Approximately 320 calories, 22g protein, 8g carbohydrates, 22g fats, 0g fiber, 55mg cholesterol, 420mg sodium, 120mg potassium per serving.

## 7.3.2. Recipe 90: "Jingle Bell Cheddar Pot"

Yield: 6 servings | Preparation time: 10 minutes | Cooking time: 15 minutes.

Ingredients:

- 200g mellow Cheddar cheese, grated
- 200g Monterey Jack cheese, grated
- 1 cup apple cider
- 2 teaspoons cornstarch
- 1/2 teaspoon mustard powder
- A pinch of paprika
- Pretzel bites, apple slices, and roasted chicken cubes for dipping

Directions:

1. Combine the apple cider, cornstarch, mustard powder, and paprika in the fondue pot and bring to a gentle simmer.
2. Gradually add in the Cheddar and Monterey Jack cheeses, stirring until they're completely melted and the pot looks like Santa's workshop come to life.
3. Serve your beautiful cheese creation with salty pretzel bites, crisp apple slices, and roasted chicken cubes.

Nutrition information:

Nutritional value: Approximately 380 calories, 23g protein, 7g carbohydrates, 28g fats, 0g fiber, 80mg cholesterol, 450mg sodium, 100mg potassium per serving.

### 7.3.3. Recipe 91: "Frosty's Swiss Wonderland"

Yield: 6 servings | Preparation time: 15 minutes | Cooking time: 20 minutes.

Ingredients:

- 300g Swiss cheese, grated
- 1 cup non-alcoholic white wine or grape juice
- 1 tablespoon lemon juice
- 2 tablespoons cornstarch
- Nutmeg and white pepper to taste
- Cubed ham, gherkins, and pearl onions for dipping

Directions:

1. Pour the non-alcoholic white wine and lemon juice into the fondue pot, heating until warm.
2. Blend the cornstarch with Swiss cheese, then gradually introduce the mixture to the pot, stirring constantly.
3. Season with nutmeg and white pepper, whisking until the fondue becomes as smooth as a fresh layer of snow.
4. Once it's ready, invite the youngsters (and adults!) to dip to their heart's content with cubed ham, gherkins, and pearl onions as accompaniments.

Nutrition information:

Nutritional value: Approximately 410 calories, 29g protein, 8g carbohydrates, 30g fats, 0g fiber, 85mg cholesterol, 660mg sodium, 150mg potassium per serving.

---

These family-friendly cheese fondue recipes promise to fill your home with warmth and cheer this holiday season. So don your Santa hats, rally the family, and dip into these cheesy delights that are sure to become new festive favorites!

## 7.4. Yuletide Twists: Global Fondue Fusions

Let's take a sleigh ride around the world, decking the halls with boughs of globally-inspired cheese fondues. From the spices of India to the robust flavors of Italy, each recipe in "Yuletide Twists" is a fusion of traditional holiday ingredients with the joyous communal spirit of fondue.

### 7.4.1. Recipe 92: "Curry Masala Melt"

Yield: 6 servings | Preparation time: 15 minutes | Cooking time: 20 minutes.

Ingredients:

- 200g paneer, cubed
- 200g Gouda cheese, grated
- 1 cup light cream
- 2 tablespoons tomato paste
- 1 tablespoon curry powder
- 1 teaspoon garam masala
- 1/2 teaspoon turmeric
- 1/4 teaspoon cayenne pepper (adjust to taste)
- Naan bread and blanched cauliflower for dipping

Directions:

1. Warm the light cream in the fondue pot over medium heat until it's hot but not boiling.
2. Stir the tomato paste and the spices into the cream until well combined.
3. Gradually add the paneer and Gouda, stirring continuously until the cheese is melted and the fondue is creamy.
4. Adjust the seasoning with cayenne pepper for a bit of heat if desired.
5. Serve with pieces of warm naan bread and florets of blanched cauliflower to bring a burst of Indian flavors to your festive table.

Nutrition information:

Nutritional value: Approximately 380 calories, 18g protein, 12g carbohydrates, 28g fats, 0.5g fiber, 90mg cholesterol, 550mg sodium, 200mg potassium per serving.

## 7.4.2. Recipe 93: "Tuscan Truffle Temptation"

Yield: 6 servings | Preparation time: 15 minutes | Cooking time: 15 minutes.

Ingredients:

- 200g Taleggio cheese, rind removed and diced
- 200g Fontina cheese, diced
- 1/2 cup whole milk
- 2 tablespoons white truffle oil
- 1/2 teaspoon garlic powder
- A pinch of Italian herbs
- Fresh parsley, chopped for garnish
- Ciabatta cubes, roasted mushrooms, and sundried tomatoes for dipping

Directions:

1. Combine milk, truffle oil, garlic powder, and Italian herbs in the fondue pot and heat gently.
2. Slowly incorporate the Taleggio and Fontina cheeses until the mixture becomes a luxurious pool of molten cheese.
3. Once it reaches the desired consistency, garnish with freshly chopped parsley.
4. Accompany with ciabatta cubes, roasted mushrooms, and sundried tomatoes to bring the flavors of an Italian Christmas into your home.

Nutrition information:

Nutritional value: Approximately 400 calories, 20g protein, 5g carbohydrates, 32g fats, 0g fiber, 85mg cholesterol, 620mg sodium, 100mg potassium per serving.

### 7.4.3. Recipe 94: "Poblano Pepper Piñata"

Yield: 6 servings | Preparation time: 20 minutes | Cooking time: 20 minutes.

Ingredients:

- 200g Asadero cheese, shredded
- 200g Oaxaca cheese, shredded
- 1 cup Mexican crema or sour cream
- 2 poblano peppers, roasted, skinned, seeded, and chopped
- 1/4 teaspoon cumin
- Fresh cilantro, finely chopped
- Tortilla strips and cooked chorizo bits for dipping

Directions:

1. Stir the sour cream or Mexican crema and cumin together in the fondue pot over medium heat.
2. Blend in the poblano peppers for a touch of smokiness and subtle heat.
3. Gradually mix in the Asadero and Oaxaca cheeses, constantly stirring until they're completely melted into a festive, stringy celebration.
4. Sprinkle with cilantro just before serving.
5. Dive into this cheesy wonder with crisp tortilla strips and spicy chorizo, embodying the lively spirit of a Mexican holiday celebration.

Nutrition information:

Nutritional value: Approximately 390 calories, 18g protein, 9g carbohydrates, 31g fats, 0.5g fiber, 95mg cholesterol, 570mg sodium, 100mg potassium per serving.

---

Embracing the holiday season with these global fondue fusions is like taking a trip around the world right from your dining table. May these recipes inspire joy, spark conversation, and deliver a kaleidoscope of flavor to your festive gatherings. Happy dipping, fellow fondue travelers!

## 7.5. Around the Fire: Outdoor Fondue Gatherings

As the chill of winter blankets the world, what could be cozier than huddling around a crackling fire under a starry sky with a fondue pot simmering nearby? Let's embrace the crisp outdoor air and transform your backyard or patio into a twinkling fondue utopia, perfect for any winter celebration.

### 7.5.1. Recipe 95: "Campfire Cheese Cascade"

Yield: 6 servings | Preparation time: 15 minutes | Cooking time: 20 minutes.

Ingredients:

- 300g Raclette cheese, shredded
- 300g Swiss cheese, shredded
- 1 garlic clove, minced
- 1 1/2 cups apple cider
- 1 tablespoon cornstarch
- 1 tablespoon apple brandy or calvados
- Salt and pepper to taste
- Cubed crusty bread, mini sausages, and pickled onions for dipping

Directions:

1. Begin by lighting your outdoor fondue burner or heating your fondue pot over the grill.
2. Add the apple cider and minced garlic to the pot, allowing it to warm up until steaming but not boiling.
3. Toss the shredded cheeses with cornstarch in a bowl to coat them lightly.
4. Gradually stir the cheese mixture into the warm cider, continuously stirring to melt the cheese uniformly.
5. Once the mixture is bubbling gently, incorporate the brandy, then season with salt and pepper.
6. Serve with rustic bread, hearty mini sausages, and tangy pickled onions, perfect for outdoor dipping and enjoyment.

Nutrition information:

Nutritional value: Approximately 440 calories, 28g protein, 12g carbohydrates, 32g fats, 0g fiber, 95mg cholesterol, 670mg sodium, 150mg potassium per serving.

**Outdoor Fondue Tips:**

1. Choose the Right Equipment: Ensure your fondue pot is suitable for outdoor use. Cast iron pots are especially good for retaining heat on chilly nights.
2. Prepare for the Elements: If it's particularly windy or cold, consider using a fondue burner with a controllable flame to keep the cheese at the perfect temperature.
3. Optimum Seating Arrangements: Arrange seats close enough to the pot for easy dipping, but with ample space to avoid any discomfort from the fire. Cozy blankets are a welcome addition to each chair.
4. Lighting and Ambiance: String up some outdoor lights or place lanterns around the seating area. Not only will this create a festive atmosphere, but it will also help guests see as they dip into the night.
5. Safety First: Keep a water source or fire extinguisher nearby just in case of an emergency, and make sure to brief your guests on the fondue pot's safe use over an open flame.

An outdoor fondue gathering combines the delights of al fresco dining with the heartwarming charm of communal cooking. So layer up, light the fire, and let the fondue fun begin!

# 7.6. The New Year's Day Brunch Fondue

After the sparkle and pop of New Year's Eve, welcome the first morning of the new year with a delightful brunch fondue. It's a perfect way to gather friends and family for a cozy start to the year, featuring lighter fondue options that will reconcile the indulgence of the festive period with the year's fresh beginnings.

## 7.6.1. Recipe 96: "Morning Mimosa Meltdown"

Yield: 6 servings | Preparation time: 10 minutes | Cooking time: 15 minutes.

Ingredients:

- 200g Brie, rind removed and cubed
- 200g Gouda, shredded
- 1 cup Champagne or sparkling wine
- 2 fresh oranges, juiced
- 1 teaspoon honey
- A pinch of cayenne pepper
- 1 baguette, cubed
- Fresh strawberries and sliced peaches for dipping

Directions:

1. In your fondue pot, gently warm the Champagne or sparkling wine and orange juice. Do not allow it to simmer or the bubbles will escape.
2. Slowly add the Brie and Gouda, stirring until the cheeses melt into a harmonious blend.
3. Add the honey and a pinch of cayenne pepper for a gentle heat and complexity.
4. Serve with fresh, crusty baguette cubes and ripe fruit - the acidity and freshness of the fruit will pair beautifully with the creamy fondue and provide a bright, cheerful start to the year.

Nutrition information:

Nutritional value: Approximately 350 calories, 20g protein, 15g carbohydrates, 20g fats, 1g fiber, 70mg cholesterol, 450mg sodium, 180mg potassium per serving.

## 7.6.2. Recipe 97: "Sunrise Chèvre Chaud"

Yield: 6 servings | Preparation time: 10 minutes | Cooking time: 10 minutes.

Ingredients:

- 300g soft goat cheese (chèvre)
- 1/2 cup milk or light cream
- 2 tablespoons apricot preserves
- 1 tablespoon chopped fresh basil
- Artisan crackers and vegetable crudités for dipping

Directions:

1. Over medium heat, warm up the milk or light cream in the fondue pot.
2. Crumble the chèvre into the pot, stirring until the cheese is melted and the mixture is smooth.
3. Stir in the apricot preserves for a hint of sweetness and the fresh basil for an aromatic lift.
4. Serve with a selection of artisan crackers and a colorful array of vegetable crudités, such as bell pepper sticks, cherry tomatoes, and carrots - a delightful combination for a laid-back brunch vibe.

Nutrition information:

Nutritional value: Approximately 330 calories, 22g protein, 8g carbohydrates, 24g fats, 0g fiber, 80mg cholesterol, 420mg sodium, 200mg potassium per serving.

Hosting a New Year's Day brunch fondue is about slow mornings, shared stories of the night before, and savoring moments of togetherness. So gather your brunch crew, prepare your palate for a delicious day ahead, and revel in the joy that only a pot of melted cheese can bring.

# 7.7. The Leftovers Revival Fondue

After the confetti has settled and the holiday roasts are enjoyed, the question that ponders in the silence of the refrigerator light is "What to do with all these leftovers?" Fret not, for 'tis the season to give your festive remnants a cheesy rebirth. Welcome to "The Leftovers Revival Fondue," where the remains of yesterday's feast become the stars of today's pot.

## 7.7.1. Recipe 98: "Post-Feast Roast Redux"

Yield: 6 servings | Preparation time: 10 minutes | Cooking time: 15 minutes.

Ingredients:

- 300g Swiss cheese, shredded
- 200g cooked roast beef or turkey, diced
- 1 cup low-sodium beef or turkey broth
- 2 teaspoons Worcestershire sauce
- 1 teaspoon horseradish sauce
- 2 teaspoons Dijon mustard
- A handful of leftover roast vegetables, diced
- Cubes of stale bread, such as the end-pieces of the holiday loaf

Directions:

1. Warm the broth gently in the fondue pot until steaming.
2. Blend in the Worcestershire sauce, horseradish, and mustard, stirring for flavor unity.
3. Gradually introduce the Swiss cheese, gently melting it into the broth and creating a velvety foundation.
4. Now, stage a comeback with the roast beef or turkey and roast veggies, letting them mingle until heated through, embracing the cheesy cascade.
5. Serve with the bread cubes, which will absorb the rich flavors and add delightful texture.

Nutrition information:

Nutritional value: Estimated based on ingredients (not including bread) for 6 servings—approximately 360 calories, 30g protein, 4g carbohydrates, 25g fats, 0g fiber, 100mg cholesterol, 420mg sodium, 250mg potassium per serving.

### 7.7.2. Recipe 99: "Holiday Ham and Swiss Swirl"

Yield: 6 servings | Preparation time: 10 minutes | Cooking time: 20 minutes.

Ingredients:

- 200g leftover holiday ham, diced
- 300g aged Swiss cheese or similar, shredded
- 1 cup milk or a mixture of milk and cream
- 2 tsp cornstarch
- A sprinkle of nutmeg and cayenne pepper
- Leftover herbed dinner rolls or garlic bread, cubed

Directions:

1. On low heat, whisk together the shredded cheese and cornstarch in the fondue pot before adding the milk, preventing clumping.
2. Stir constantly until the cheese melts into a blissful pool.
3. Season with nutmeg and a gentle whisper of cayenne pepper for a little kick.
4. Toss in the ham and let it get acquainted with the cheese, warming up to its former glory.
5. Cubed rolls or garlic bread — perhaps a bit dry from their time on the counter — now find purpose, becoming the ideal vessels for the hearty fondue.

Nutrition information:

Nutritional value: Estimated based on ingredients (not including bread) for 6 servings—approximately 380 calories, 32g protein, 5g carbohydrates, 27g fats, 0g fiber, 85mg cholesterol, 520mg sodium, 200mg potassium per serving.

---

These leftover revival fondues are not just recipes; they are a celebration of resourcefulness and the acknowledgment that good food deserves an encore. Open the fridge, gather your remains of feasts past, and let's ensure that this holiday cheer extends far beyond the final toast. Here's to giving leftovers a delicious and dignified curtain call in the fondue pot!

## 7.8. Pairing and Sharing: Festive Drinks and Fondue

In the spirituous splendor of festive occasions, nothing complements the communal caress of a cheese fondue better than the embracing clink of glassware, brimming with holiday elixirs. From heartening cocktails to merry wines and spirited concoctions, let's unwrap the secrets to the perfect libations for each cheesy dip.

## Mulled Marvels and Vino Verities

The very essence of yuletide in a cup, mulled wine, with its mulling spices and citrus zests, makes for a heartfelt companion to any cheese fondue. Opt for lighter, fruit-forward red wines if mulling from scratch, or select a bottle of pre-made cheer for convenience.

- Fondue Friend: Traditional Swiss or Alpine-style fondue pot.
- Pairing Perk: The spices in the wine echo the nutmeg often found in fondue, creating a seamless palate experience.

## Bubbly Bliss

Champagne and sparkling wines aren't merely for toasting but offer an effervescent cutting through the richness of the fondue.

- Fondue Friend: A New Year's Eve Bubbly Cheese Pot.
- Pairing Perk: The bubbles and crisp acidity in Champagne clean the palate, making each dip as delightful as the first.

## Crafty Concoctions

Artisanal beers and craft ales offer a tapestry of flavors—from hoppy IPAs to malty stouts—that can stand up to robust and hearty fondue mixtures.

- Fondue Friend: Cheddar and stout fondue variations.
- Pairing Perk: The toasted notes of a good stout resonate deeply with the savory aspect of the cheese.

## Holiday Cocktails

Cocktails such as eggnog, spiced rum punches, or cinnamon whisky sours can bring warmth and spice to match the convivial atmosphere of fondue dipping.

- Fondue Friend: Cheese fondue infused with seasonal spices or spirits.
- Pairing Perk: Cocktails customized with holiday flavors bring an additional dimension of festivity to each fondue bite.

## Non-Alcoholic Nog and Punch

Not to overlook non-alcoholic options, spiced apple cider and non-alcoholic eggnog let everyone join the cheers, encapsulating holiday essence in a family-friendly form.

- Fondue Friend: Family-friendly cheese fondues with mild and creamy cheeses.

- Pairing Perk: These drinks keep the holiday spirit timeless and inclusive, allowing all to cherish the warmth of the occasion.

### Tea Traditions

Holiday teas, whether a robust black tea to mimic the tannins of wine or a soothing herbal blend, can offer a refined and calming accompaniment to your fondue feast.

- Fondue Friend: Light cheese fondues aimed for brunch or daytime gatherings.
- Pairing Perk: Tea offers a soothing counterbalance to the indulgence of cheese and satisfies the palate with every sip.

As you gather around the fondue pot with your loved ones, let the shared drinks be the toast to moments past and the sip into future memories. May the merriment of your pairings only be rivaled by the joy of your company. Cheers, Salud, Prost, and Joyeux Noël!

# 7.9. Fondue Party Games: Holiday Edition

As the cheese begins to flow and the spirits glow, what could be more splendid than a dash of competitive spirit to add zest to your gathering? Within "Fondue Party Games: Holiday Edition," we unfold a charming catalogue of fondue-centered merriment, fit for all who have congregated to dip and delight.

### The Dip and Dare

Each guest takes a turn to dip their morsel into the molten pot; should their piece of bread or fruit fall off into the cheese, they must then undertake a holiday dare. Dares can range from singing a carol, sharing an embarrassing holiday tale, or performing a jolly jig.

- For the Young Elves: Simplify the dares into challenges like "name five reindeer" or "do your best Santa laugh."

### Who's Who in the Winterland

Each guest draws a card with the name of a holiday character or item. Without looking at their own card, they stick it onto their forehead, and the game begins. They must ask yes or no questions, trying to identify who or what they "are" as they make their dips.

- Festive Twist: Combine the guesswork with fondue dipping—only after a successful dip into the pot can a question be asked.

**Fondue Pictionary**

Draw from a bowl of holiday-themed prompts and have each guest or team sketch their prompt in the air, using the fondue fork as a pointer while the others guess. Just remember, no double-dipping your fork afterward!

- For the Snowy Scribbles: Provide a whiteboard or paper for a more traditional Pictionary game, with bonus points for drawing with a fondue stick!

**Melting Memories**

This game invites reminisces of the fondue past. Go around the circle and have each person share a favorite holiday memory before they dip. Once a complete round is made, guests must recall one detail from each story shared.

- For Sweet Recollections: Encourage children to talk about their favorite present or holiday food and see if the adults can remember.

**Pass the Parcel... With a Fondue Twist!**

Wrap a small gift multiple times and pass it around as music plays. When the music stops, the person holding the gift unwraps a layer. Inside each layer, place a paper with a number that dictates how many dips a person has to make in succession for everyone else.

- Cheesy Surprises: In some layers, include fondue-themed challenges, like creating the tallest cheese string or naming a cheese for every letter in their name.

**The Great Fondue Quiz**

Devise a holiday-themed quiz complete with cheese and fondue facts. Questions can be asked throughout the evening, and for every correct answer, guests earn a special kind of cheese for an extra dip or a festive drink refill.

- Kid's Corner: Include child-friendly questions about holiday stories, characters, and songs so they can earn fun toppings for their dippers.

With these games in play, your fondue party is assured to be bubbling with laughter, camaraderie, and a pinch of festive competition. So grab your fondue fork and let the games begin! May the best dipper win, and may the holidays be ever jubilant!

# Chapter 8: "Green and Lean: Vegetarian and Dietary Fondue"

Welcome, dear fondue lovers, to a verdant feast that is as kind to your body as it is to the Earth. Picture a pot where the cheese's golden hues are reminiscent of a sunset, only lighter on the palate and the conscience. This is "Green and Lean," a chapter dedicated to those who tread lightly but indulge heartily. Here, there's reverence for the vegetarian way of life, a bow to dietary diversities, and a celebration of the sheer possibilities in the realm of mindful eating.

Whether you have adopted a full vegetarian lifestyle, are exploring dietary options, or simply wish to incorporate more plant-powered meals into your life, this chapter serves as your guide to a fondue experience that is as inclusive as it is innovative. We're stripping back the indulgence to showcase the vibrant, nutritious, and mouthwatering delights that vegetarian and dietary-conscious fondue can offer.

So gather your freshest produce, your most flavorful non-dairy cheeses, and your zest for culinary creativity—because Fondue is about to get a green and lean makeover.

## 8.1. Verdant Vats: Vegetable Broth Fondue

Immerse yourself in the nutritious and savory depths of vegetable broth fondue. This is where health meets heartiness, robust flavors meet gentle cooking, and the bounty of the garden becomes the star of your dining table.

### 8.1.1. Recipe 100: "Garden Harvest Brew"

Yield: 6 servings | Preparation time: 10 minutes | Cooking time: 20 minutes.

Ingredients:

- 32 ounces vegetable broth, homemade or good quality store-bought
- 1/4 cup dry white wine or non-alcoholic wine
- 2 garlic cloves, minced
- 1 teaspoon dried herbs (thyme, oregano, or a blend)
- 1 tablespoon olive oil
- A medley of vegetables for dipping (such as blanched broccoli, cherry tomatoes, sliced bell peppers, and mushrooms)
- Cubed crusty whole-grain bread or gluten-free bread, if preferred

Directions:

1. Heat olive oil in your fondue pot over medium heat. Add minced garlic and sauté until fragrant.
2. Pour in the vegetable broth and white wine, bringing the mixture to a gentle simmer. Infuse with dried herbs.
3. Adjust the heat on your fondue pot to maintain a simmer without boiling, keeping all the delicate flavors and aromas alive.
4. Arrange an assortment of fresh, crisp veggies and bread around the pot.
5. Invite guests to skewer their favorite vegetables and bread, then dip into the herbed broth, enjoying the infusion of garden goodness in each bite.

Nutrition information:

Nutritional value ( does not include dippers): Approximately 50 calories, 1g protein, 3g carbohydrates, 3.5g fats, 0g fiber, 0mg cholesterol, 200mg sodium, 180mg potassium per serving.

Gather around the glow of your fondue pot, where the warmth of shared company and the joy of healthful eating collide. Here in "Green and Lean," we nourish not only our bodies but also our spirits with every dip.

## 8.2. Fromage sans Fromage: Dairy-Free Delights. The Quest for Non-Dairy Nirvana

Venture we now into the realm of the dairy-free — a realm where cheese is not cheese and the plant-based heart finds its delight. Enter "Fromage sans Fromage," a gallant quest to transform the essence of plant-derived wonders into fondues that even the staunchest cheese aficionados would bless with a nod of approval. These recipes craft the delectable paradox of cheeseless cheese pots, bubbling with all the jubilation of their dairy counterparts.

### 8.2.1. Recipe 101: "The Avocado Avo-lution Dip"

Yield: 4 servings | Preparation time: 20 minutes | Cooking time: 10 minutes.

Ingredients:

- 2 ripe avocados, peeled and pitted
- 1 cup unsweetened almond milk
- 2 tablespoons nutritional yeast
- 1 teaspoon tapioca starch
- 1/2 teaspoon garlic powder
- 1 tablespoon lime juice
- 1/2 teaspoon cumin

- Fresh cilantro, chopped
- Assorted raw veggies, gluten-free bread, and tortilla chips for dipping

Directions:

1. In a blender, purée the avocados with almond milk, nutritional yeast, tapioca starch, garlic powder, lime juice, and cumin until smooth.
2. Pour the mixture into a fondue pot and gently heat, stirring frequently until it slightly thickens and is warmed through.
3. Garnish with fresh cilantro and serve with a colorful array of your favorite dippable veggies, gluten-free bread, and crispy tortilla chips for a creamy experience that defies the dairy decree.

Nutrition information:

Nutritional value: Approximately 232 calories, 5g protein, 14g carbohydrates, 19g fats, 7g fiber, 0mg cholesterol, 86mg sodium, 712mg potassium per serving.

## 8.2.2. Recipe 102: "Cashew Cauldron Creaminess"

Yield: 4 servings | Preparation time: 15 minutes | Cooking time: 10 minutes.

Ingredients:

- 1 1/2 cups raw cashews, soaked overnight and drained
- 3/4 cup water
- 1/4 cup nutritional yeast
- 1 tablespoon lemon juice
- 1 clove garlic
- 1/2 teaspoon onion powder
- 1 tablespoon miso paste (ensure gluten-free if necessary)
- Roasted potatoes, mushrooms, and asparagus tips for dipping

Directions:

1. Blend soaked cashews, water, nutritional yeast, lemon juice, garlic, onion powder, and miso paste until absolutely smooth and creamy.
2. Transfer the cashew mixture to a fondue pot and cook over low heat, stirring until the fondue thickens to a dippable consistency.
3. If the mixture is too thick, add a splash of more water until the desired consistency is reached.
4. Serve with an assortment of roasted potatoes, earthy mushrooms, and asparagus tips, perfect for encapsulating the flavors into every dip.

Nutrition information:

Nutritional value: Approximately 312 calories, 10g protein, 18g carbohydrates, 24g fats, 2g fiber, 0mg cholesterol, 182mg sodium, 593mg potassium per serving.

---

With "Fromage sans Fromage," audience to the rich reality that dairy-free can indeed be delightful and delicious, we salute the innovative spirit that makes fondue a dish for all — sans dairy, sans compromise, sans equal. Enjoy these dairy-free delights and let the dipping commence!

# 8.3. Slim Sauce: Low-Calorie Fondues

Embark on a culinary journey where indulgence meets mindfulness. "Slim Sauce: Low-Calorie Fondues" invites you to savor the delectable world of fondue without the post-dip guilt. This chapter unveils the art of creating lighter fondues that dazzle the taste buds while keeping the waistline in a joyful repose.

**Subtle Swaps and Crafty Cuts**

- Trim the Fat: Opt for reduced-fat cheeses and skimmed milk bases, cutting the calories without losing the creamy essence of fondue.
- Broth Bases: Use a savory vegetable or chicken broth as a fondue base to bathe your dippers in flavor without the weight of heavy creams or full-fat cheeses.
- Veggie Volume: Bulk up the pot with nutrient-dense, fiber-rich vegetables like spinach, kale, or tomatoes that absorb the cheesy goodness and boost the health factor.
- Lean Meats: Consider incorporating lean proteins such as white-meat chicken or turkey as a satiating, low-calorie dipper option.

## 8.3.1. Recipe 103: "Featherlight Fromage Feast"

Yield: 6 servings | Preparation time: 15 minutes | Cooking time: 10 minutes.

Ingredients:

- 200g reduced-fat Swiss cheese, grated
- 100g reduced-fat Cheddar cheese, grated
- 2 cups skimmed milk
- 2 tablespoons low-calorie cream cheese
- 1 tablespoon flour
- 2 teaspoons lemon juice
- Salt and pepper to taste
- Sliced bell peppers, carrots, and whole-wheat bread cubes for dipping

Directions:

1. Blend the grated Swiss and Cheddar with flour in a bowl and set aside.
2. In a fondue pot, gently heat the skimmed milk and cream cheese until hot but not boiling.
3. Gradually whisk in the flour-coated cheese until melted and smooth.
4. Add lemon juice, followed by salt and pepper, for that zing and zest.
5. Present with slices of crisp bell peppers, crunchy carrots, and cubes of whole-wheat bread to dip into the light but luscious concoction.

Nutrition information:

Nutritional value: Approximately 200 calories, 18g protein, 9g carbohydrates, 9g fats, 1g fiber, 30mg cholesterol, 340mg sodium, 200mg potassium per serving.

## 8.3.2. Recipe 104: "Garden Gala Dip"

Yield: 6 servings | Preparation time: 10 minutes | Cooking time: 15 minutes.

Ingredients:

- 400g silken tofu
- 1/2 cup vegetable broth
- 1/4 cup nutritional yeast
- 1 teaspoon garlic powder
- 1 tablespoon white miso paste
- 1 tablespoon Dijon mustard
- A pinch of turmeric for color
- Crudités and apple slices for dipping

Directions:

1. In a blender, puree the silken tofu with vegetable broth until silky.
2. Transfer the blend to a fondue pot, stirring in nutritional yeast, garlic powder, miso paste, mustard, and turmeric.
3. Cook over a gentle heat, stirring continuously until the mixture is hot and thickened.
4. Surround with an array of crudités—think colorful vegetables like radishes, cucumber, and snap peas, plus crisp apple slices for a touch of sweetness.

Nutrition information:

Nutritional value: Approximately 80 calories, 7g protein, 4g carbohydrates, 3g fats, 2g fiber, 0mg cholesterol, 210mg sodium, 120mg potassium per serving.

Discover that lightness in fondue is not a stern regime but a playful and pleasurable adaptation, threading through the same sense of warmth and community as its traditional counterpart. The Slim Sauce chapter is not a list of limitations, but an expansive menu of possibilities. So, dine in delectation, knowing each dip is as kind to your palate as it is to your calorie count.

# 8.4. Gluten-Free Gratification: No Bread, No Problem!

In the land where cheese flows as freely as rivers, a gluten-free guest should never have to experience the famine of fun. Let's lift the veil on a world where the gluten is gone but the gratification is plentiful. Welcome to "Gluten-Free Gratification," where the dipping delights are as inclusive as they are delectable.

### The Art of Alternative Dippers

- The Road Less Bready: Venture beyond the usual bread cubes and embrace an array of gluten-free dippers. From crisp vegetables to fluffy gluten-free focaccia, the options are diverse and delicious.
- Cracker Chronicles: Gluten-free crackers come in a myriad of flavors and textures. Whether seeded, herbed, or nut-flavored, they provide the perfect sturdy vehicle for cheesy ventures.
- Fruitful Dipping: Fresh fruits like sliced apples, pears, and firm peaches offer a sweet contrast to the savory richness of the cheese.

## 8.4.1. Recipe 105: "Gluten-Free Gruyère Glide"

Yield: 6 servings | Preparation time: 15 minutes | Cooking time: 15 minutes.

Ingredients:

- 400g Gruyère cheese, grated
- 1 cup dry white wine (ensure it's gluten-free)
- 1 tablespoon gluten-free cornstarch
- 1 garlic clove, minced
- 2 tablespoons kirsch (make sure it's gluten-free)
- A pinch of nutmeg
- Gluten-free bread, cubed
- Blanched broccoli and cauliflower for dipping

Directions:

1. In a fondue pot, bring the wine and garlic to a gentle simmer—watch for bubbles but ward off boiling.
2. Mix the cornstarch with kirsch in a separate bowl until dissolved.

3. Gradually add the Gruyère into the simmering wine, stirring with a wooden spoon in a figure-eight motion until melted and smooth.
4. Stir the cornstarch mixture into the cheese and keep stirring until it thickens to that coveted fondue consistency.
5. Season with a whisper of nutmeg, then serve with cubes of gluten-free bread and blanched broccoli and cauliflower florets.

Nutrition information:

Nutritional value: Approximately 370 calories, 28g protein, 5g carbohydrates, 27g fats, 0g fiber, 100mg cholesterol, 620mg sodium, 100mg potassium per serving.

## 8.4.2. Recipe 106: "Cheesy Chickpea Bonanza"

Yield: 6 servings | Preparation time: 20 minutes | Cooking time: 10 minutes.

Ingredients:

- 200g soft goat cheese
- 200g feta cheese, crumbled
- 1/2 cup milk (or a non-dairy alternative if preferred)
- 2 tablespoons chickpea flour
- 1 teaspoon dried oregano
- Gluten-free flatbread or pita, cut into pieces
- Cherry tomatoes and snap peas for dipping

Directions:

1. Whisk chickpea flour into milk in your fondue pot and warm the mixture over low heat until it starts to thicken.
2. Add in the goat cheese and feta, continuing to whisk until you've got a smooth mixture.
3. Sprinkle in the oregano for a Mediterranean flair.
4. Once the fondue is velvety and warm, it's ready for dipping. Serve alongside gluten-free flatbread or pita and a vibrant selection of cherry tomatoes and fresh snap peas.

Nutrition information:

Nutritional value: Approximately 310 calories, 22g protein, 11g carbohydrates, 21g fats, 1g fiber, 65mg cholesterol, 870mg sodium, 200mg potassium per serving.

---

In "Gluten-Free Gratification," we affirm that gluten-free doesn't equate to joy-free. With these recipes, those who navigate the gluten-free seas can savor every cheesy journey with gusto, sipping from the fondue pot of flavor and community with no breaded borders.

119

# 8.5. Protein-Packed Pots: Meatless and Mighty

In the verdant fields of vegetarian vigor, we find our Protein-Packed Pots, brimming with meatless marvels that staunchly defy the notion that only meat can muster muscle. Here, we pay tribute to the powerhouses of the plant kingdom, presenting fondues that are both meatless and mighty, ensuring that every dip is a dive into a pool of nourishing delight.

**Tofu Triumphs and Lentil Laurels**

- Bean Curd Bounty: Gently poached silken tofu becomes a sponge for your fondues, gracefully soaking up flavors while providing a protein-packed bite.
- Lentil Legends: A dalliance with delicately spiced lentil patties can offer a surprising, filling twist to the dipping tradition.

## 8.5.1. Recipe 107: "Soy and Savor Soirée"

Yield: 4 servings | Preparation time: 15 minutes | Cooking time: 15 minutes.

Ingredients:

- 200g silken tofu, cut into cubes
- 200g extra-firm tofu, pressed and cubed
- 1 cup vegetarian dashi or vegetable broth
- 2 tablespoons soy sauce or tamari for a gluten-free option
- 1 teaspoon sesame oil
- 1 garlic clove, minced
- Spring onions and sesame seeds for garnish
- Steamed edamame, rice balls, and mushroom caps for dipping

Directions:

1. Warm the vegetarian dashi in the fondue pot, embellished with soy sauce, sesame oil, and minced garlic.
2. Once a gentle simmer is achieved, introduce the silken and extra-firm tofu, allowing the pieces to poach and infuse with flavor.
3. Serve the fondue crowned with a sprinkling of sliced spring onions and a scatter of sesame seeds for an added textural experience.
4. Pair with a platter of steamed edamame, tightly packed rice balls, and savory mushroom caps to round out this ode to the noble soybean.

Nutrition information:

Nutritional value: Approximate calculations per serving, tofu and broth only—160 calories, 14g protein, 6g carbohydrates, 9g fats, 1g fiber, 0mg cholesterol, 760mg sodium, 200mg potassium.

## 8.5.2. Recipe 108: "Legume Lagoon"

Yield: 4 servings | Preparation time: 20 minutes | Cooking time: 20 minutes.

Ingredients:

- 200g red lentils, cooked and mashed
- 200g chickpeas, cooked and mashed
- 1 cup unsweetened almond milk
- 2 tablespoons nutritional yeast
- 1 tablespoon tahini
- 1/2 teaspoon ground cumin
- Salt and pepper to taste
- Gluten-free bread cubes, vegetable skewers, and falafel balls for dipping

Directions:

1. Combine almond milk, nutritional yeast, and tahini in the fondue pot and warm over a low heat, ensuring not to boil.
2. Stir in the mashed lentils and chickpeas until well-mixed and heated through.
3. Season with cumin, salt, and pepper, adjusting for flavor as you stir to a smooth consistency.
4. Invite guests to skewer gluten-free bread cubes, vegetables, and falafel, diving into the pot's rich, creamy legume landscape.

Nutrition information:

Nutritional value: Approximate calculations per serving, legumes and almond milk only—190 calories, 11g protein, 24g carbohydrates, 6g fats, 8g fiber, 0mg cholesterol, 300mg sodium, 320mg potassium.

---

With these "Protein-Packed Pots," we celebrate the might of meatless options, proving that a world of hearty, fulfilling indulgences awaits in the vegetarian realm. Gather all for a communal dip that warms the soul and nourishes the body with every delightful, protein-rich plunge.

# 8.6. The Organic Oasis: Clean and Conscious

Journey with us to "The Organic Oasis," where the focus is on the purity of the pot. Here, organic isn't just a label—it's a culinary philosophy, a commitment to the natural and the unadulterated, ensuring that every ingredient that graces the fondue pot is as clean and conscious as the mountain spring.

## 8.6.1. Recipe 109: "Earth's Embrace Gruyère Fondue"

Yield: 4 servings | Preparation time: 20 minutes | Cooking time: 15 minutes.

Ingredients:

- 300g organic Gruyère cheese, grated
- 200g organic Emmental cheese, grated
- 1 garlic clove, organically grown, minced
- 1 and 1/2 cups organic white wine, such as a Chardonnay
- 1 tablespoon organic cornstarch
- 2 tablespoons organic kirsch
- Freshly ground organic pepper and a pinch of nutmeg
- Organic bread cubes, cherry tomatoes, and young carrots for dipping

Directions:

1. In your fondue pot, swirl together the white wine and garlic on a gentle heat until warm, letting the aromas meld.
2. Combine the grated cheeses with the cornstarch in a separate bowl.
3. Gradually introduce the cheese mixture into the wine, stirring ceaselessly with a wooden spoon to welcome a smooth consistency.
4. Once the cheeses are entirely enchanted into the wine, ripple through the kirsch, and season with pepper and nutmeg.
5. Dip into this wholesome concoction with an array of organic dippers—bread bites fresh from the local baker, sweet tomatoes, and crisp carrots from the farmers' market.

Nutrition information:

Nutritional value: Approximate calculations per serving, cheeses and wine only—400 calories, 28g protein, 5g carbohydrates, 28g fats, 0g fiber, 90mg cholesterol, 250mg sodium, 100mg potassium.

## 8.6.2. Recipe 110: "Whole Earth Herb Havarti"

Yield: 4 servings | Preparation time: 15 minutes | Cooking time: 10 minutes.

Ingredients:

- 400g organic Havarti cheese, grated
- 1 cup organic vegetable broth
- 2 tablespoons organic apple cider vinegar
- 1 tablespoon organic all-purpose flour
- 1/4 cup organic herbs (such as basil, dill, and chives), finely chopped
- Organic whole grain bread, blanched cauliflower, and apple slices for dipping

Directions:

1. In the cauldron of the fondue pot, simmer the vegetable broth infused with apple cider vinegar.
2. Toss the Havarti with flour to create a veil of protection before gently sprinkling it into the pot.
3. A verdant shower of herbs is next, folded in to steep their healing essences into the cheese.
4. Serve with heart-happy options like whole grain bread, the earth's own cauliflower, and apples crisp with autumn's kiss.

Nutrition information:

Nutritional value: Approximate calculations per serving, cheeses and broth only—350 calories, 23g protein, 5g carbohydrates, 26g fats, 0g fiber, 80mg cholesterol, 220mg sodium, 80mg potassium.

---

In "The Organic Oasis," we honor the integrity of the ingredients, cherishing their stories—from the farm where no pesticides dwell to the table where conviviality abounds. These recipes remind us that a fondue party can be both a feast and an homage to the nurturing earth that provides.

## 8.7. Flavor Without Fuss: Simple and Sensible Fondue Recipes

In the land of simplicity, we find joy in the understated, the elegant, the effortlessly refined. Let us journey through "Flavor Without Fuss," where fondue exudes pure essence and uncomplicated charm. These recipes are a tribute to minimalism, designed for those with sensitive diets or a preference for culinary clarity, where fewer ingredients speak volumes.

### 8.7.1.Recipe 111: "Simply Swiss Serenity"

Yield: 4 servings | Preparation time: 10 minutes | Cooking time: 15 minutes.

Ingredients:

- 400g high-quality Swiss cheese, grated
- 1 cup dry white wine (such as a Swiss Fendant)
- 1 teaspoon cornstarch
- A pinch of grated nutmeg
- Cubed gluten-free bread and steamed new potatoes for dipping

Directions:

1. Warm the white wine gently in the fondue pot—enough for whispers of steam but no tempestuous boils.
2. Dust the grated cheese with cornstarch and thread it gradually into the warmed wine, weaving a tapestry of silken cheese as you stir.
3. Allow this simple mixture to become one with itself, melting into serene smoothness.
4. A hint of nutmeg graces the fondue like snow on the Alps, stirring in this final, fragrant flourish before the feast begins.
5. Present with gluten-free bread—crisped on the outside, tender within—and steamed new potatoes, their earthy wholesomeness ready for a dip.

Nutrition information:

Nutritional information is estimated for cheese fondue made with Swiss cheese and wine for 4 servings: Approximately 380 calories, 24g protein, 4g carbohydrates, 25g fats, 0g fiber, 85mg cholesterol, 180mg sodium, 75mg potassium.

### 8.7.2. Recipe 112: "Seductively Simple Spinach Soak"

Yield: 4 servings | Preparation time: 10 minutes | Cooking time: 20 minutes.

Ingredients:

- 300g fresh baby spinach, washed and finely chopped
- 2 cups low-fat milk or unsweetened almond milk
- 200g feta cheese, crumbled
- White pepper and a squeeze of lemon to taste
- Carrot sticks, radishes, and cucumbers for dipping

Directions:

1. In a trusty fondue pot, summon the milk to just below a simmer, a stage set for the subtle drama of melting.
2. Unto this pot, introduce the spinach, watching the green leaves wilt into the warm bath.
3. Crumble in the feta, allowing its soft demeanor to disperse amidst the spinach swirl.
4. Season with but a whisper of white pepper and a tender squeeze of lemon—a brightening note in this gentle chorus.
5. Serve alongside a troupe of fresh vegetables, their crispness a perfect contrast to the mellow fondue.

Nutrition information:

Nutritional information is estimated for spinach and feta fondue made with low-fat milk for 4 servings: Approximately 220 calories, 19g protein, 9g carbohydrates, 12g fats, 2g fiber, 45mg cholesterol, 380mg sodium, 450mg potassium.

---

Each of these "Flavor Without Fuss" fondues is a sonnet to simplicity, an ode to digestion-friendly dining, and a testament to the grace of less-is-more. May they bring peace to your table and a gentle satisfaction to your soul.

## 8.8. Festive Fodmap-Friendly Fondues

For many, the merry jingle of holiday bells rings in tandem with the need for mindful eating. In "Festive Fodmap-Friendly Fondues," we weave a tapestry of recipes that sidestep common digestive triggers without sacrificing the communal cheer that comes with a pot of fondue. Unite around the warmth of a shared meal with dishes designed to be kind to all, gifting comfort and care in every bite.

**Low-FODMAP Fondue Etiquette**

- Harness the power of low-lactose cheeses, and befriend the gentleness of green tips, from scallions and chives, avoiding the more robust white bulbs.
- Celebrate the inclusion of gluten-free grains, rescuing dipping options from the grips of dietary restrictions.

## 8.8.1. Recipe 113: "Gentle Gourmet's Gouda and Grapes"

Yield: 4 servings | Preparation time: 15 minutes | Cooking time: 20 minutes.

Ingredients:

- 200g aged Gouda cheese (naturally lower in lactose), grated
- 200g lactose-free mozzarella cheese, grated
- 1 cup lactose-free or almond milk
- 1 tablespoon garlic-infused olive oil (FODMAP friendly)
- 2 tablespoons cornstarch mixed with water to form a slurry
- Grapes, orange bell peppers, and gluten-free bread for dipping

Directions:

1. Drizzle the garlic-infused oil into the fondue pot, slowly warming to infuse the flavor without releasing any offending FODMAPs.
2. Stir the almond milk in and bring to a gentle shimmer—a soft and welcoming heat.
3. Gradually incorporate the Gouda and mozzarella cheeses that have been previously bathed with cornstarch, until smooth.
4. Serve with a playful arrangement of grapes, sliced bell peppers, and gluten-free bread, providing a FODMAP-friendly feast that is both digestibly content and joyfully indulgent.

Nutrition information:

Nutritional value: Estimated per serving (cheese and almond milk only, excluding dipping items)—300 calories, 20g protein, 5g carbohydrates, 22g fats, 0g fiber, 60mg cholesterol, 430mg sodium, 100mg potassium.

## 8.8.2. Recipe 114: "Fructose-Free Fondue Frolic"

Yield: 4 servings | Preparation time: 15 minutes | Cooking time: 20 minutes.

Ingredients:

- 150g Pecorino Romano cheese, finely grated

- 150g Swiss cheese, grated
- 1 cup chicken broth (homemade or certified low FODMAP)
- 1 tablespoon chives, chopped
- 1 tablespoon dill, chopped
- 1 tablespoon Dijon mustard (check for additives)
- Carrot sticks, cucumber, and rice crackers for dipping

Directions:

1. In the fondue pot, bring the chicken broth to a simmer, a low toiling, ready to welcome the cheeses into its embrace.
2. Whisk in the Swiss cheese and Pecorino, summoning them to melt uniformly and without resistance.
3. A pinch of chopped chive and dill, before you even ponder the existence of the mustard—a gentle squeeze, and then a stir through the molten milieu.
4. Present with pride crisp vegetable sticks and rice crackers, the FODMAP warriors of crunch, to dive and dance within the pot's fructose-free fountain.

Nutrition information:

Nutritional value: Estimated per serving (cheese and chicken broth only, excluding dipping items)—320 calories, 24g protein, 4g carbohydrates, 24g fats, 0g fiber, 85mg cholesterol, 450mg sodium, 100mg potassium.

---

In this chapter, the goal is not only to nourish but to nurture, offering up fondues that all can enjoy with abandon. Here, the spirit of the holiday season finds expression in the kindness of our recipes, proving that it is indeed possible to feast festively while respecting each diner's dietary path.

## 8.9. Indulgence Inside the Lines: Allergy-Aware Fondues

Navigating the joyful seas of fondue dining requires a keen eye for those who embark on the journey with specific dietary needs. "Indulgence Inside the Lines" casts a light upon allergy-aware fondues that circumnavigate common allergens, charting a course for safe and inclusive culinary pleasures. In this sanctuary, every guest can dive into the fondue pot with confidence and glee.

**Allergen Almanac: Mapping Out Safe Waters**

- Dairy Detours: Explore the realm of plant-based cheeses that ensure those with dairy allergies can enjoy a fondue experience without concern.
- Nut-Free Novelties: Carefully select ingredients from trusted sources to ensure no cross-contamination, keeping the fondue nut-free and nurturing.
- Gluten-Free Graces: Earmark gluten-free recipes that champion alternative bread and dippers, giving those with sensitivities the freedom to dip to their heart's content.

## 8.9.1. Recipe 115: "Safe Harbor Swiss-style Fondue"

Yield: 4 servings | Preparation time: 20 minutes | Cooking time: 15 minutes.

Ingredients:

- 200g dairy-free Swiss cheese alternative, shredded
- 200g dairy-free mozzarella cheese alternative, shredded
- 1 cup unsweetened rice milk
- 2 tablespoons nutritional yeast
- 2 teaspoons tapioca starch mixed with water to create a slurry
- 1 teaspoon lemon juice
- Pinch of mustard powder
- Salt to taste
- Gluten-free bread cubes, blanched asparagus, and apple slices for dipping

Directions:

1. In the vigilant vessel of the fondue pot, warm the rice milk while whispering in the lemon juice and mustard powder until combined.
2. Gradually introduce the cheese alternatives, stirring steadily, as they willingly acquiesce to melt into unity.
3. With the grace of patience, add the slurry of tapioca starch, guiding the fondue to a desired silky enclave.
4. Season with a pinch of salt and serve alongside gluten-free bread, asparagus, and apples—honored dippers in our allergy-aware assembly.

Nutrition information:

Nutritional value: Estimated per serving (with dairy-free cheese and rice milk only, excluding dippers)—Approximately 280 calories, 5g protein, 20g carbohydrates, 20g fats, 0g fiber, 0mg cholesterol, 640mg sodium, 30mg potassium.

### 8.9.2. Recipe 116: "Peaceful Peanut-free Pimento Dip"

Yield: 4 servings | Preparation time: 15 minutes | Cooking time: 20 minutes.

Ingredients:

- 300g pimento cheese spread, certified nut-free
- 1/2 cup chicken or vegetable broth, nut-free and gluten-free
- 1/4 teaspoon smoked paprika
- 1/4 teaspoon garlic powder
- Vegetable sticks (such as carrots, celery, and bell peppers)
- Nut-free and gluten-free crackers for dipping

Directions:

1. In the protective embrace of the fondue pot, blend the nut-free pimento cheese spread with the broth, heating gently to encourage togetherness.
2. Season this blossoming relationship with smoked paprika and a hint of garlic powder, stirring to a culinary communion.
3. Display an array of colorful vegetable sticks and nut-free, gluten-free crackers for the dipping pleasure of your cherished crew.

Nutrition information:

Nutritional value: Estimated per serving (pimento cheese and broth only, excluding dippers)—Approximately 200 calories, 9g protein, 5g carbohydrates, 16g fats, 0.5g fiber, 40mg cholesterol, 450mg sodium, 175mg potassium.

---

Embrace this guide as a compass for navigating allergy-aware dining, wherein the details are tended with care and every guest can immerse themselves in the shared jubilation of fondue. Remember, the art of fondue is not just in the melting; it's in the moment—one that's made safe, delicious, and inclusive for all in attendance.

In the cozy corners of the world, where the glow of a single candle flickers on the face of adoration, we find our ninth chapter, a romantic repast for duos in dining. "Twosome Tableau" is an intimate ballet of flavors where fondue becomes the centerpiece of a dance meant for two. Whether it's a date night, an anniversary, or simply a shared moment in time, these recipes are resized and reimagined to cater to coupledom's culinary connection.

# Chapter 9: "Twosome Tableau: Fondue for Two"

- A tender prelude to taste shared between two hearts. A glimpse into the ways fondue can be the meal that not only fills the belly but also fuels the flames of amour.

## 9.1. Let's dive into a romantic fondue experience designed for a cozy night in.

### 9.1.1. Recipe 117:Svelte Alpine Night

Yield: 2 servings | Preparation time: 10 minutes | Cooking time: 15 minutes.

Ingredients:

- 150g Gruyère cheese, grated
- 150g Emmental cheese, grated
- 1 garlic clove, peeled
- 1/3 cup dry white wine, such as a Swiss Fendant or a crisp Sauvignon Blanc
- 1/2 tablespoon lemon juice
- 1/2 tablespoon cornstarch
- 1 tablespoon kirsch (optional)
- A pinch of freshly grated nutmeg
- Freshly ground black pepper to taste
- A small baguette, cubed, and lightly steamed vegetables, for dipping

Directions:

1. Begin by cutting the garlic in half and rubbing the inside of the fondue pot with the cut sides to infuse it with flavor. Discard the garlic afterward.
2. Pour the white wine and lemon juice into the pot and warm over medium heat until bubbles form on the surface but not boiling.
3. In a small bowl, toss the grated cheeses with the cornstarch until they are evenly coated. This helps to stabilize the cheese and prevent oiliness.
4. Gradually add the cheese to the pot a handful at a time, stirring constantly in a smooth figure-eight pattern to encourage even melting.
5. Once the cheese has melted and the fondue is smooth, stir in the kirsch, if using.
6. Season with nutmeg and black pepper to your liking.
7. Serve with cubes of baguette and an array of lightly steamed vegetables, like broccoli florets and carrot sticks.

Nutrition information:

Nutritional value: Approximately 560 calories, 36g protein, 22g carbohydrates, 34g fats, 1g fiber, 169mg cholesterol, 366mg sodium, 108mg potassium per serving.

---

This fondue merges the cherished traditions of the Alpine fondue with a portion perfect for two. Nestle into the night, let the cheese bubble and the wine glasses clink and enjoy each dip as the snow falls quietly outside. Here's to a "Svelte Alpine Night" that warms the heart as much as the hearth.

## 9.1.2. Recipe 118:Choco-Berry Whisper

Yield: 2 servings | Preparation time: 10 minutes | Cooking time: 5 minutes.

Ingredients:

- 4 ounces high-quality dark chocolate, roughly chopped
- 1/3 cup heavy cream
- 1 tablespoon honey or to taste
- A splash of vanilla extract
- A pinch of salt
- Fresh strawberries, sliced
- Raspberries and blackberries
- Marshmallows and cubes of pound cake for dipping

Directions:

1. In a small saucepan, gently heat the heavy cream over a low flame until it's just starting to steam—keep an eye out to ensure it doesn't boil.
2. Remove from the heat and add the chopped dark chocolate, whisking heartily until the chocolate has fully melted and the mixture is lustrous and seamless.
3. Stir in the honey—for just the right whisper of sweetness—the vanilla extract, and a pinch of salt to elevate the chocolate's profundity.
4. Pour the rich chocolate fondue into a shared pot designed for two or individual ramekins for personal dipping bliss.
5. Serve immediately with a platter of fresh strawberries, raspberries, and blackberries, skewered marshmallows, and tender cubes of pound cake, ready to be baptized in chocolate.

Nutrition information:

Nutritional value: Approximately 480 calories, 4g protein, 45g carbohydrates, 32g fats, 4g fiber, 35mg cholesterol, 85mg sodium, 365mg potassium per serving.

---

For a night steeped in the melody of muted conversations and the soft rustle of falling rose petals, "Choco-Berry Whisper" brings a symphony of simple pleasures. There's a magic in the pairing of chocolate with the tart sweetness of berries—each dipping moment, a ballet of the senses, each taste, a promise of yet more delights to come.

### 9.1.3. Recipe 119:Tipsy Twosome and Tipsy Cheddar

Yield: 2 servings | Preparation time: 15 minutes | Cooking time: 10 minutes.

Ingredients:

- 150g sharp Cheddar cheese, grated
- 2 tablespoons cornstarch
- 1/2 cup lager or ale, room temperature
- 1 teaspoon Worcestershire sauce
- 1/2 teaspoon dry mustard powder
- 1 garlic clove, minced
- A pinch of cayenne pepper
- Cubed multigrain bread and blanched vegetables (such as cauliflower florets and sliced bell peppers) for dipping

Directions:

1. In a bowl, toss the grated Cheddar in cornstarch until it is well-coated. This will help stabilize the cheese and create a smooth fondue.
2. Rub the inside of the fondue pot with the minced garlic clove for a hint of piquancy, then pour in the beer and gently warm it over medium heat; be careful not to boil.
3. Gradually incorporate the Cheddar into the warmed beer, continually stirring until the cheese is melted and the mixture bonds into a harmonious brew.
4. Stir in the Worcestershire sauce and dry mustard powder for added depth of flavor and a touch of cayenne for a slight heat that whispers rather than roars.
5. Once the mixture is velvety, serve it up with cubes of heart-healthy multigrain bread and a selection of freshly blanched vegetables.

Nutrition information:

Nutritional value: Approximately 400 calories, 22g protein, 12g carbohydrates, 28g fats, 0g fiber, 80mg cholesterol, 620mg sodium, 68mg potassium per serving.

---

This "Tipsy Twosome and Tipsy Cheddar" fondue is a toast to cozy nights and the intimate cheer shared between two people. Each dunk into the ale-infused pot is not just about savoring the sharp undertones of Cheddar but also about reveling in the company of your beloved companion. Cheers to love, to laughter, and to a cheese fondue that gently tips the heart!

## 9.2."Candlelit Classics"

In the softly lit corners of the culinary world, where flickering flames cast a gentle glow on expectant faces, lies the elegance of classics. "Candlelit Classics" features fondue recipes that have stood the test of time, refined and reimagined for a duo's intimate evening. Rekindle the flame with these scaled-down recipes that promise a night of shared whispers and savored bites.

### 9.2.1. Recipe 120: "Intimate Emmental and Gruyère Embrace"

Yield: 2 servings | Preparation time: 10 minutes | Cooking time: 15 minutes.

Ingredients:

- 100g Emmental cheese, shredded
- 100g Gruyère cheese, shredded
- 1 garlic clove, halved
- 1/2 cup dry white wine (preferably a variety like Fendant)
- 1/2 tbsp lemon juice
- 1/2 tbsp cornstarch
- 1/2 tbsp kirsch (optional)
- Pinch of ground nutmeg
- Freshly ground black pepper
- French baguette, cubed, and steamed baby carrots or green beans for dipping

Directions:

1. Rub the fondue pot with the cut sides of the garlic clove to infuse the flavor, then discard the garlic.
2. Pour in the white wine and lemon juice, warming over medium heat until just steaming.

3. Toss together the cheeses and cornstarch in a bowl, ensuring an even coat.
4. Gradually add the cheese mixture into the pot, stirring constantly in an arching figure-eight motion for even melting.
5. If using, blend in the kirsch at this point.
6. Finalize with a pinch of nutmeg and a grind of black pepper, stirring gently.
7. Serve with cubes of French baguette and a selection of steamed vegetables, ready for a tender dip in the velvety cheese.

Nutrition information:

Nutritional value: Approximately 450 calories, 28g protein, 6g carbohydrates, 34g fats, 0g fiber, 100mg cholesterol, 280mg sodium, 100mg potassium per serving.

## 9.2.2. Recipe 121: "Chocolate Fondue for Two"

Yield: 2 servings | Preparation time: 5 minutes | Cooking time: 5 minutes.

Ingredients:

- 4 oz quality dark chocolate, broken into pieces
- 1/3 cup heavy cream
- 1 tbsp brown sugar (optional, depending on the sweetness of the chocolate)
- A small dash of pure vanilla extract
- A pinch of sea salt
- Fresh strawberries, sliced bananas, and marshmallows for dipping

Directions:

1. In a saucepan over low heat, warm the heavy cream with the brown sugar if you're using it.
2. Once the cream is warm and the sugar has dissolved, turn off the heat and add the dark chocolate, allowing it to sit for a moment before stirring until smooth.
3. Stir in the vanilla extract and the pinch of sea salt, mixing thoroughly.
4. Pour the decadent chocolate mixture into a fondue pot set over a gentle flame.
5. Present with an assortment of strawberries, banana slices, and marshmallows for a sweet, timeless indulgence.

Nutrition information:

Nutritional value: Approximately 400 calories, 4g protein, 36g carbohydrates, 28g fats, 4g fiber, 40mg cholesterol, 100mg sodium, 500mg potassium per serving.

"Candlelit Classics" brings the time-honored traditions to a size that's just right for an evening of two. As these classic recipes make their way from the pot to the palate, may they kindle the softest of conversations and light the warmest of smiles. Here's to the classics, and to the enduring love they celebrate.

## 9.3. Seduction by Dippers

In the intricate dance of fondue dining, the dippers serve as the alluring accompaniment to the main act. No rendezvous around the fondue pot is complete without the perfect ensemble of dippers, poised to seduce both the eyes and the palate. Here we offer a selection of dippers that not only tantalize the taste buds but also allure with their aesthetic grace.

### Artisanal Bread Basket

A basket of carefully chosen bread is the cornerstone of any fondue spread. Select an assortment that offers different textures and flavors:

- Charred Ciabatta: Grilled until crispy with visible grill marks, adding a touch of smoky sophistication.
- Walnut Baguette Slices: Elegantly sliced with a nutty crunch, offering an unexpected texture.
- Olive Focaccia: Infused with savory Mediterranean accents, presenting hues of green and purple amidst the golden crust.

### Garden's Bounty

Fresh vegetables, when chosen with care, transcend their supporting role and can become stars in their own right:

- Endive Leaves: These chic, boat-shaped leaves are perfect for scooping and add a pleasantly bitter crispness.
- Asparagus Spears: Lightly grilled with a drizzle of olive oil and a sprinkle of salt, turning each dip into a luxe delight.
- Cherry Tomato Skewers: Sweet, vibrant, and artfully threaded onto miniature skewers, perfect for a single swoop through the cheese.

### Bountiful Orchard

No tableau is as enticing as the lush offerings from the orchard, prepared to perfection:

- Fig Halves: Soft and sweet, their delicate nature and jammy interior pair divinely with rich, creamy cheeses.
- Sliced Pears: With their buttery flesh and gentle sweetness, they beckon seductively to swirls of Gorgonzola.
- Apple Roses: Thinly sliced and rolled into rose shapes, dedication to beauty and a moment's audition for the fruit's crisp freshness.

**Farm Stand Charms**

From local farm stands, pick the finest to charm and seduce:

- Pickled Carrots: Sweet and tangy, with a crunch that resonates long after the dip.
- Baby Beetroot: Roasted, halved, and adorned with a dollop of goat cheese prior to dunking, adding depth and richness.

**Aphrodisiac Additions**

Some say that certain foods ignite the embers of passion. Whether or not this rings true, their addition to your fondue can but only entice:

- Chocolate-Dipped Strawberries: Feeding one another these after a cheese fondue can weave an air of romance into the evening.
- Chili-Infused Pineapple: A spicy twist upon the tropical tang, with the heat purportedly fanning the flames of desire.

With "Seduction by Dippers," every choice is an invitation, a culinary caress, beckoning to a night of shared glances and flavors in whispers. Let each dip be the prelude to the memories you'll craft, together, fondue fork in hand, indulgence heartily planned.

# 9.4. Bubbly and Cheese

Whisk away your cherished companion to a place where effervescent elixirs meet the molten wonders of cheese. "Bubbly and Cheese" is a testament to the luxurious union of sparkling wines with fondue, each sip heralding the fizz of celebration, the pop of potential; a pairing guide dedicated to lovers and dreamers dining à deux.

**The Sparkling Spectrum**
- Vivacious Veuve with Classic Swiss: The crispness of a Veuve Clicquot Champagne cleanses the palate and cuts through the richness of a traditional

Swiss fondue. A playful interaction of textures and flavors, where robust meets refined.

- Playful Prosecco with Mozzarella Marvel: Prosecco's light, fruity notes are a delightful counterpoint to the creamy gentleness of a mozzarella-based fondue, turning the dining experience into a cheerful symphony.
- Cuddlesome Cava with Smoky Gouda: The bubbly embrace of Spanish Cava wraps itself around a fondue infused with the heady aroma of smoked Gouda, striking a suave balance between overt flavors and subtle undertones.

### The Art of Pairing

Choosing the right bubbly for your cheese fondue is akin to selecting the perfect piece of music for a romantic evening:

- For the Bold and Beautiful: Pair potent cheese fondues, laden with flavors like blue cheese or aged Cheddar, with a robust Champagne such as Pinot Noir-heavy blends which can match the intense taste profiles.
- The Light and Lively: For fondues that favor the mild and creamy cheeses like Brie or Camembert, opt for a lighter sparkling wine, like a Brut Prosecco or a crisper Brut Cava, known for their subtle fruitiness and uplifting presence.
- Sweet Whispers: For chocolate or dessert fondues, consider a demi-sec Champagne or a Moscato d'Asti with its sweet effervescence that can elevate the sweetness of the chocolate while adding its own whispered hints of romance to the evening.

### In Each Bubble, a World

Remember, the pairing of bubbly and cheese fondue is not just about taste but about the experience—the clinking of glasses, the shared smiles, and the effervescent joy that each bubble brings to the surface. So unwind the wire cage, let the cork fly, pour into flutes, and raise a toast to twosomes everywhere.

With "Bubbly and Cheese," may the only thing more sparkling than your drink be the gleam in each other's eyes. Cheers to love, to fondue, and to a pairing as timeless as romance itself.

## 9.5. Melt of the Moment

In the heartbeats between the past and the infinite possibilities, lies the "Melt of the Moment." This is where contemporary renditions of fondue come to play, painting the canvas of now with rich, decadent flavors, each pot a mix of adventure and the comfort of shared connection.

When you aim to choreograph a special memory, let these modern twists on classic fondue guide you through a sensual culinary experience. Let the dance of the artisan blue cheese with a honey drizzle begin, and the smoky undertones of a spiced gouda fondue entice the senses.

## 9.5.1. Recipe 122: "Honeyed Blue Cheese Euphoria"

Yield: 2 servings | Preparation time: 10 minutes | Cooking time: 10 minutes.

Ingredients:

- 150g creamy blue cheese, crumbled
- 1/4 cup heavy cream
- 2 tablespoons milk
- 1 tablespoon honey, plus extra for drizzling
- Fresh thyme leaves for garnishing
- Pear slices, walnut bread cubes, and blanched green beans for dipping

Directions:

1. In a fondue pot, combine the heavy cream, milk, and honey, warming over low heat.
2. Add the crumbled blue cheese, stirring gently until it melds into the creamy base.
3. Once the mixture achieves a smooth, united front, remove from heat.
4. Drizzle with additional honey and sprinkle fresh thyme leaves atop.
5. Serve with pear slices that complement the blue cheese tang, walnut bread for its hearty crunch, and green beans for their fresh snap.

Nutrition information:

Nutritional value: Estimated per serving—320 calories, 14g protein, 15g carbohydrates, 24g fats, 0g fiber, 75mg cholesterol, 650mg sodium, 200mg potassium.

## 9.5.2. Recipe 123: "Whisper of Smoked Gouda Bliss"

Yield: 2 servings | Preparation time: 15 minutes | Cooking time: 15 minutes.

Ingredients:

- 200g smoked Gouda, grated
- 1/2 cup milk
- 1/2 teaspoon smoked paprika
- 1/4 teaspoon garlic powder
- Pinch of cayenne pepper
- Grilled chorizo slices, roasted red peppers, and crusty bread for dipping

Directions:

1. In a fondue pot, introduce milk and warm it gently with a care not to boil.
2. Gradually incorporate the smoked Gouda, stirring until each shred has patiently surrendered to the warmth.
3. Season with smoked paprika, garlic powder, and a daring pinch of cayenne.
4. When the cheese has capitulated into velvety smoothness, the fondue is ready.
5. Accompany the fondue with grilled chorizo slices whose spice will echo the Gouda's smokiness, roasted red peppers for a subtle sweetness, and bread that stands strong against the molten tide.

Nutrition information:

Nutritional value: Estimated per serving—410 calories, 22g protein, 12g carbohydrates, 32g fats, 0g fiber, 105mg cholesterol, 720mg sodium, 180mg potassium.

---

Let "Melt of the Moment" be the culinary artist of your special occasions. With these seductive and contemporary fondue recipes, each moment shared around the pot becomes a brush stroke on the canvas of memory, a mingling of flavors and sentiments that will linger long after the final dip.

# 9.6. Recipes for Romance

In the delicate theater of amour, where each gesture and glance weave together to form the tapestry of affection, "Recipes for Romance" stands as a testament to love's sweet cadence. These fondue recipes are the edible equivalent of a lover's sonnet, where flavors, aromas, and textures interlace to craft a sensory serenade for two souls entwined.

### 9.6.1. Recipe 124: "Ardent Asiago and Artichoke Amore"

Yield: 2 servings | Preparation time: 10 minutes | Cooking time: 15 minutes.

Ingredients:

- 200g Asiago cheese, finely grated
- 1/2 cup dry rosé wine
- 2 tablespoons marinated artichoke hearts, finely chopped
- 1/2 teaspoon Italian seasoning
- A drizzle of truffle oil (optional for a luxurious touch)
- Salt and fresh cracked black pepper to taste
- Rosemary focaccia bread cubes and roasted cherry tomatoes for dipping

Directions:

1. In your fondue vessel of love, simmer the rosé wine gently, evoking the pink blush of romance.
2. Whisk the Asiago cheese into the wine, adding it with adoration until it surrenders into smoothness.
3. Stir in the artichoke hearts as tenderly as one would fold a love letter, dusting with Italian seasoning for additional poetry.
4. If you choose, finalize with a graceful drizzle of truffle oil, bringing intimacy to the flavors akin to a whispered secret.
5. Season with salt and a dance of pepper, then serve accompanied by the herbaceous embrace of rosemary focaccia and the sweet char of roasted cherry tomatoes.

Nutrition information:

Nutritional value: Estimated per serving—420 calories, 28g protein, 5g carbohydrates, 33g fats, 0g fiber, 67mg cholesterol, 1024mg sodium, 92mg potassium.

## 9.6.2. Recipe 125: "Brie and Berries Ballet"

Yield: 2 servings | Preparation time: 5 minutes | Cooking time: 10 minutes.

Ingredients:

- 150g Brie cheese, rind removed and cubed
- 100g fresh raspberries, plus extra for garnish
- 1/4 cup champagne
- A sprinkle of edible rose petals (optional for garnish)
- Brioche toast points and dark chocolate pieces for dipping

Directions:

1. Into the warm cocoon of the fondue pot, pour the champagne, a bubbly beginning to a tender tale.
2. Add the Brie cubes, slowly melting them under a low flame, less like cooking and more like letting the cheese awaken to its own velvety potential.
3. Once melted, introduce the raspberries, marrying the creaminess of the cheese with the fruit's delicate tartness.
4. Serve with brioche points for their sweet softness and squares of dark chocolate, because what whispers romance better than chocolate?
5. As a crowning touch, garnish with fresh raspberries and edible rose petals, a visual sonnet to accompany the taste.

Nutrition information:

Nutritional value: Estimated per serving—390 calories, 19g protein, 20g carbohydrates, 27g fats, 2g fiber, 95mg cholesterol, 700mg sodium, 200mg potassium.

---

Let each "Recipe for Romance" serve as a stanza in your evening's sonnet, a chapter in your night's novel. Picture the two of you, a quiet corner, the glow of a single candle — and the fondue pot, a shared cauldron of love's own crafting, savor between stories and storied moments yet to come.

## 9.7. Sweets for the Sweet

Dessert is not merely the final act of a meal but the lasting impression, the tender sweetness that lingers like a gentle kiss farewell. It's the poetic pause that prolongs a pleasurable experience, and what better encore than a dessert fondue meant for sharing? "Sweets for the Sweet" offers dessert fondues crafted to kindle joy and romance, transforming a simple night into an exquisite memory.

### 9.7.1. Recipe 126: "Dark Decadence and Fruit Fantasia"

Yield: 2 servings | Preparation time: 10 minutes | Cooking time: 5 minutes.

Ingredients:

- 6 oz dark chocolate (70% cacao), finely chopped
- 1/2 cup heavy cream
- 2 tablespoons orange liqueur or orange juice
- A pinch of ground cinnamon
- Fresh berries (strawberries, raspberries, blackberries)

- Banana slices and orange segments for dipping
- Homemade marshmallows or angel food cake for an added touch of sweetness

Directions:

1. In a small saucepan, heat the cream until it begins to simmer. Be cautious not to let it boil over, much like one's restrained anticipation of sweetness.
2. Turn off the heat and add in the dark chocolate, whisking steadily as it succumbs to the cream's embrace, melting into a smooth oblivion.
3. Gently stir in the orange liqueur and sprinkle of cinnamon, weaving in zest and spice.
4. Pour the concoction into a fondue pot, letting the low flame caress the bottom and keep the chocolate warm and ready.
5. Serve with an assortment of fresh fruits, each ready to dip and be transformed by the chocolate, and squares of angel food cake that soak up the fondue with a celestial lightness.

Nutrition information:

Nutritional value: Estimated per serving—400 calories, 4g protein, 25g carbohydrates, 34g fats, 5g fiber, 30mg cholesterol, 35mg sodium, 400mg potassium.

## 9.7.2. Recipe 127: "Caramel Cream Dream"

Yield: 2 servings | Preparation time: 10 minutes | Cooking time: 10 minutes.

Ingredients:

- 1/3 cup caramel sauce
- 1/4 cup heavy cream
- 1 tablespoon dark rum or apple cider (optional)
- Sea salt flakes for a touch of contrast
- Granny Smith apples, pretzel sticks, and buttery pound cake for dipping
- Chopped toasted nuts (such as pecans or hazelnuts) for garnish

Directions:

1. Combine caramel sauce and heavy cream in your fondue pot, stirring them over a gentle heat.
2. Once the mixture flows smoothly, like liquid gold, stir in the dark rum for depth or apple cider for an autumnal note.
3. The caramel fondue should be warm and tempting, a sweet siren calling.

4.  Dip in crisp apple slices for a jolt of tartness, pretzel sticks for crunch and savoriness, or chunks of pound cake for pure indulgence.
5.  Sprinkle with sea salt flakes, which make the sweetness pop, and garnish with toasted nuts for an earthy undercurrent.

Nutrition information:

Nutritional value: Estimated per serving—300 calories, 2g protein, 25g carbohydrates, 22g fats, 1g fiber, 40mg cholesterol, 180mg sodium, 120mg potassium.

---

In "Sweets for the Sweet," may you find the endearing embrace of shared sweetness and the lingering flavors of affection. Unveil these sweet fondues with your partner, and let the sensorial voyage draw you closer as you dip and discover layer after layer of luscious delight. Here's to the desserts that capture the heart and the moments that captivate the soul.

# 9.8. Love Potions and Libations

When fondue is shared by two, the experience transcends mere dining; it becomes a soiree of the senses. "Love Potions and Libations" presents a curated selection of beverages designed to harmonize with fondue's warm embrace. These exquisite sips, from fine wines to crafted cocktails, are poured with the intention of enhancing the mood and the meal.

**Wine Whispers**
1.  Pinot Noir: A versatile and delicate red wine that pairs lovingly with the savory undertones of cheese fondue without overpowering the palate.
2.  Riesling: Whether you opt for dry or sweet, the high acidity and fruity undertones of a Riesling complement both cheese and chocolate fondues.
3.  Champagne: For chocolate fondue, a brut Champagne adds a pop of celebratory finesse, while its crispness contrasts beautifully with the silkiness of melted cheese.

**Cocktail Caresses**
4.  Elderflower Spritz: A gentle blend of elderflower liqueur with sparkling wine, topped with a splash of soda water, pairs wonderfully with light and creamy fondues.

5. Classic Martini: Choose a gin or vodka martini with a twist of lemon to cut through the richness of the cheese and cleanse the palate between dips.
6. Bourbon Old Fashioned: The smooth, warming notes of bourbon and bitters alongside a hint of sweetness offer a sturdy counterbalance to bold fondue flavors.

## Non-Alcoholic Elixirs

7. Sparkling Grape Juice: The effervescence of chilled sparkling grape juice provides a festive touch suitable for all, mirroring the qualities of a fine Champagne.
8. Lavender Lemonade: Handcrafted lavender lemonade offers a fragrant floral touch that's refreshing alongside the umami depth of cheese.
9. Iced Mint Tea: A cool glass of mint tea can be especially palate-cleansing and soothing when enjoying the richer notes of a chocolate fondue.

## Savor in Sync

Remember, the beauty of "Love Potions and Libations" is in the interplay between sip and dip. Each drink should be a sonnet that celebrates the momentary flavors of fondue, while each fondue bite awaits the echo of the libation's reply. These libations are not mere drinks but the silent narrators of your love story, enriching each chapter with taste and tenderness. Cheers to moments sipped, love savored, and memories that, like the finest wines and elixirs, will only grow richer with time.

# 9.9. Nocturne of Nourishment

In a celebration of health and harmony, we convene under the "Nocturne of Nourishment," where dietary mindfulness waltzes with epicurean delight. Let this chapter be your guide to a fondue experience that is rich in care, freedom, and flavor while honoring well-being as the soirée's cherished guest.

## An Ode to Vitality

Just as the moon nurtures the night, our nourishment-focused fondue nurtures the body. Here, healthful ingredients and allergy-friendly choices ensure that dietary restrictions never dim the luster of a fondue evening.

## 9.9.1. Recipe 128: "Hearts Aflame Avocado Fondue"

Yield: 2 servings | Preparation time: 10 minutes | Cooking time: 15 minutes.

Ingredients:

- 1 ripe avocado, mashed
- 1 cup unsweetened almond milk
- 2 tablespoons nutritional yeast for a cheese-like flavor
- 1 teaspoon arrowroot powder or tapioca starch for thickening
- 1 garlic clove, finely minced
- A squeeze of lemon juice
- Salt and a dash of chili flakes to taste
- Fresh vegetables such as steamed broccoli, carrot sticks, and bell pepper strips for dipping

Directions:

1. Begin by whisking the arrowroot or tapioca starch into the almond milk until fully dissolved.
2. Warm the mixture in your fondue pot, adding the nutritional yeast and garlic, whispering a promise of flavor into the night.
3. Fold the mashed avocado into the pot, watching as the creamy green melds with the zesty concoction.
4. Brighten the arcadia of avocado with a fresh squeeze of lemon juice, a seasoning of salt, and a courageous dash of chili flakes.
5. Surround the pot with a tapestry of vibrant vegetables, each one thrilled to plunge into the nourishing nectar.

Nutrition information:

Nutritional value: Approximate calculations per serving, not including vegetables— 160 calories, 5g protein, 11g carbohydrates, 12g fats, 6g fiber, 0mg cholesterol, 150mg sodium, 500mg potassium.

## 9.9.2. Recipe 129: "Alpine Essence Edamame Dip"

Yield: 2 servings | Preparation time: 10 minutes | Cooking time: 10 minutes.

Ingredients:

- 1 cup shelled edamame, cooked and pureed
- 1/2 cup low-sodium vegetable broth
- 2 tablespoons coconut cream
- 1 teaspoon miso paste, ensuring it's gluten-free
- Salt and black pepper to adjust flavors
- A sprinkle of dried wakame seaweed
- Gluten-free rice crackers and cucumber rounds for dipping

Directions:

1. In the fondue pot, mix the vegetable broth with the coconut cream, warming the liquid to a gentle tidepool of heat.
2. Introduce the edamame puree, stirring in the tide of green with the patience of a gardener nurturing seedlings.
3. Allow the miso paste to dissolve and integrate, bringing its savory soul harmoniously into the mix.
4. Season with a privilege of salt and a humble twist of black pepper, sprinkling wakame seaweed atop for a briny whisper of the sea.
5. Accompany this verdant vessel with crisp rice crackers and cool cucumber rounds, each an island adrift in this sea of green goodness.

Nutrition information:

Nutritional value: Approximate calculations per serving, not including dipping items—150 calories, 8g protein, 9g carbohydrates, 10g fats, 3g fiber, 0mg cholesterol, 210mg sodium, 370mg potassium.

---

In these recipes lie an homage to health—where taste meets well-being, and indulgence meets improvement. Let "Nocturne of Nourishment" cradle your evening in thoughtful care, wrapping each bite in the assurance of good health and the serenity of safe dining. Here's to your health, and to the joyous journey of fondue, forever savored and shared.

# 9.10. Anecdotes in Aroma

Let us waltz into a world where scents are the storytellers and spices the narrators, where the olfactory essence of fondue becomes as integral to the experience as the taste itself. In "Anecdotes in Aroma," we unveil the secrets of harnessing aromatic herbs and spices to not only enhance the fondue's flavor but also to adorn the air with enchanting fragrances that heighten the intimate ambiance.

### Herbs: The Whispering Leaves
- Rosemary: Its piney freshness brings to mind an alpine breeze, perfect with robust cheeses, and as an aromatic garnish, it's akin to kindling woodsy tales of mountainside romance by the fire.
- Thyme: The subtle, earthy quality of thyme's tiny leaves imbues lighter cheese fondues with the gentle stirrings of a herb garden at dawn, caressing the palate with every dip.

- Basil: The sweetheart of herbs, basil, when chiffonaded and stirred into a mozzarella and tomato fondue, turns each mouthful into a verse of an Italian love song.

**Spices: The Intrepid Explorers**
- Cinnamon: A mere sprinkle can transform a chocolate fondue, making each mouthful a saga of spice routes traveled and exotic lands explored.
- Nutmeg: Just a grating is like a shared secret, its warm, nutty aroma enhancing cheese fondue with a hint of comfort and nostalgia perfect for a romantic night.
- Cayenne: For those who favor a little fire, cayenne's heat elevates a fondue's flavor profile, igniting the senses and warming the soul akin to a passionate flamenco dance.

**The Olfactory Stage Setting**

Harmonizing the aromatic herbs and spices with your fondue not only pleases the palate but also contributes to an all-encompassing sensory tableau. When planning the fondue, consider:

- Decor: Including fresh sprigs of herbs like rosemary or lavender amongst the table setting, doubling as a decorative element and a natural air freshener.
- Preparation: Releasing aromas through gentle heating such as toasting spices before adding them to your pot or muddling fresh herbs in room-temperature wine.
- Serving: Offering each guest a sprig of fresh herb to rub between their fingers before eating, invoking the full scent profile and making the dining experience interactive and memorable.

**Immersive Experiences**
- Aromatherapy Pairing: For a truly immersive experience, coordinate your fondue with aromatherapy candles or diffusers. A lavender-scented candle with a mild, herbaceous fondue, or a citrus-scented one to pair with a fruit chocolate fondue, enhances the mood and the dining experience.

"Inhale deeply," whispers "Anecdotes in Aroma." Let your senses guide you through a fondue journey where every scent tells a story, every sniff a prelude to delight, creating an unforgettable tableau of aromatic indulgence.

# Chapter 10: "The Grand Finale: A Fondue Ovation"

Gather 'round, fondue faithfuls and melted cheese mavens, for we have whisked and whirled, dipped and twirled through the fondue universe, unearthing its secrets, from the steamy summits of Swiss Alps to the chocolatey depths of decadent desserts. "The Grand Finale: A Fondue Ovation" is not merely a closing curtain but a standing ovation for the journey we've taken and the culinary craft we've awakened.

**Fond Farewell or the Beginning?**

As this book's pages thin and the pots cool, do not fret, for in your hands you hold not an end, but an epicurean elixir ready to transform any gathering into a bubbling bash of bliss. See, dear reader, you're no longer a mere spectator in the art of fondue; you are now a masterful maestro, a connoisseur of the cheese pull, a siren of the swirling chocolate sea.

**To the FoTndue Faithfuls,**

Remember these essential edicts as you venture forth:

- Heat, but do not haste: Fondue, like love, cannot be rushed. It must be coaxed and caressed into being.
- The texture is paramount: Seek the silken, shun the stringy. For fondue is a ballet, and lumps are as much a faux pas as a ballerina's stumble.
- Flavor is your muse: Worship at the altar of taste, mixing, matching, and melding with wild culinary abandon.
- Aromatics are your chorus: Let them sing, let them soar, filling both room and palate with olfactory harmony.
- Dippers, the chorus line: Vary them, spice them, select them with care. They are the instruments to your melody, the partners to your fondue dance.
- To pair is to ponder: May your libations lift your spirits as your cheese lifts your forks.
- Simplicity, the sweetest note: Not every pot needs the bells and whistles; sometimes, the cheese stands alone.
- Health, your hidden guest: Honor it, embrace it, and weave it into every concoction.
- Allergy awareness, your guiding star: Navigate with it, and ensure everyone basks in the fondue glow, carefree and content.


*To Those Who've Tasted and Tested,*

If your heart swells with cheese-laden joy and your mind brims with chocolate-coated creativity, take a moment, dear reader, to pen your thoughts. Journey to Amazon, as if on a quest for rare and fine Gruyère, and leave us a review as glowing as a heated fondue pot. Share your tales of triumphs and troubleshoots, for your words could light the way for fellow travelers in the fondue fellowship.

To every fondue enthusiast who now looks upon the world with a melty middle and a hunger for more, I say: Bon appétit, bon voyage, and may the cheese be ever in your favor.

# The And

Made in the USA
Monee, IL
13 September 2024

65705124R00090